TACTICAL
PISTOL
MARKSMANSHIP

"My troops are good and well-disciplined, and the most important thing of all is that I have thoroughly habituated them to perform everything that they are required to execute. You will do something more easily, to a higher standard, and more bravely when you know that you will do it well."

Frederick the Great, *Principes Generaux*, 1748

GABE SUAREZ

TACTICAL PISTOL

MARKSMANSHIP

PALADIN PRESS · BOULDER, COLORADO

HOW TO IMPROVE YOUR COMBAT SHOOTING SKILLS

Also by Gabriel Suarez:
The Combative Perspective:
 The Thinking Man's Guide to Self-Defense
Tactical Advantage:
 A Definitive Study of Personal Small-Arms Tactics
Tactical Pistol:
 Advanced Gunfighting Concepts and Techniques
Tactical Rifle:
 The Precision Tool for Urban Police Operations
Tactical Shotgun:
 The Best Techniques and Tactics for Employing the Shotgun
 in Personal Combat

Tactical Pistol Marksmanship:
 How to Improve Your Combat Shooting Skills
by Gabe Suarez

Copyright © 2001 by Gabe Suarez

ISBN 10: 1-58160-278-2
ISBN 13: 978-1-58160-278-4
Printed in the United States of America

Published by Paladin Press, a division of
Paladin Enterprises, Inc.
Gunbarrel Tech Center
7077 Winchester Circle
Boulder, Colorado 80301 USA
+1.303.443.7250

Direct inquiries and/or orders to the above address.

PALADIN, PALADIN PRESS, and the "horse head" design
are trademarks belonging to Paladin Enterprises and
registered in United States Patent and Trademark Office.

Visit our Web site at www.paladin-press.com

TABLE OF
CONTENTS

WARNING

Firearms are potentially dangerous and must be handled responsibly by individual trainees and experienced shooters alike. The technical information presented here on firearms handling, training, and shooting inevitably reflects the author's beliefs and experience with particular firearms and training techniques under specific circumstances that the reader cannot duplicate exactly. Therefore, this book is presented *for academic study only*. It is not intended to serve as a replacement for professional instruction under a qualified firearms instructor.

PREFACE

This book is not about pistols. Rather, it is a book about how to become an accomplished shooter. Most specifically, it's intended as a companion text to my first book, *The Tactical Pistol*. In that book, I told you what needs to be done. In this book, I show you exactly how to do it.

As you read, you will notice that there is little discussion of such issues as mind-set, tactics, and tactical applications. There are many other volumes on those topics, the best of which are listed in Appendix C. This is a book about skill development. I will discuss many new concepts in pistol shooting, and I will give you a training program that will make you a better shooter. A bold statement? Perhaps, but the results will speak for themselves. The basic concepts and training drills described herein form the basis of the training programs used in many world-class shooting schools where I, and many of my colleagues, have taught in past years. Some of the material is accepted knowledge in the industry, but much of it is new.

These foundational skills, which many shooters do not understand, are essential to hitting your adversary before he hits you. Make no mistake: an elderly home defender, a citizen with a concealed carry permit, or a high-speed/low-drag operator must rely on the fundamental skills to hit their targets, lest they miss and are themselves hit. When your tactics fail (and eventually they will), the only thing standing between you and a grim future will be your marksmanship skills.

I've given you all the "secrets" here. The rest is up to you. You cannot take a magic pill and become a world-class gunfighter, any more than you can become a world-class anything that way. It takes hours of effort, gallons of sweat, and yes, maybe even a little blood. In this book, I've shown you where to focus your efforts. Study with an open mind, and practice the drills. I suspect that you will notice a big improvement in your shooting within a short period of time.

—Gabe Suarez
Southern California

ACKNOWLEDGMENTS

As usual, no book is the work of a single individual. There are a number of individuals who provided "pieces of the puzzle" through the years and who've contributed greatly in the development and understanding of many of these concepts.

First of all, I must mention my friend and pistolcraft mentor, Col. Jeff Cooper. I began training with Colonel Cooper in the late 1980s, and the knowledge I gained from him was not only the foundation of my pistol skills but also the stuff that actually saved my life on a few occasions.

I must also thank my wife, Cheryl, who has endured the best and the worst. Finally, and perhaps most of all, I must thank my friends at Paladin Press for their help and assistance with my many writing endeavors.

CHAPTER 1

HISTORICAL
PERSPECTIVE

As we stand at the threshold of a new millennium, we see that the human race has not changed much in the last 3,000 years. The things that motivate us today are the same things that motivated our hairy ancestors in the dim past. Times certainly do change, but people and their motivations do not. Julius Caesar, for example, would be incredulous at the sight of an M1 Abrahms tank rolling into battle, but he would completely understand the motivations of its operators.

Humans are, for the most part, noble and good, but they are also quite capable of unspeakable acts. The history of man is the story of one man's or one nation's aggression against another. Since our forebears first ventured down from the trees, men have been fighting to take what they desired from their weaker neighbors or to protect that which was theirs from the oftentimes stronger marauder. This was true in the green wooded past, and it is true in our concrete and asphalt present.

In ancient (and not so ancient) times, the physically strongest often carried the day. But that all changed with the invention of gunpowder and its application in the firearm. With the gun as a hand-held weapon, man had a tool whereby the weak could overcome the strong or the few could overcome the many.

The pistol has been a part of the fighting man's tool kit for several hundred years, but relatively recent developments have enabled it to reach its zenith of utility.

Early weapons were unreliable and clumsy artifacts by modern standards. The one-shot-and-reload concept did not offer much of an advantage. After the shooter fired his first shot, he was either forced to reload (time consuming and very difficult) or things deteriorated to the Stone Age tactics of hacking and slashing.

Then, in the 1830s, a man named Samuel Colt developed a reliable repeating handgun, the Colt Paterson. Based on the concept of a rotating cylinder loaded with six charges, the "revolving pistol" allowed the shooter several tries at his man before the need to reload. It was the first serious fighting handgun, and it served as a research platform from which better and more reliable weapons evolved.

With the new century came the development of smokeless

Technical advancements have been part of the reason for its success. (Photo courtesy of Chuck Taylor.)

powder and, subsequently, the semiautomatic pistol. Twentieth century warriors were quick to note that these "new" weapons had some distinct advantages over the older single- and double-action revolving pistols. The revolver, however, as Colt's original concept became known as, was not yet obsolete.

America grew ever more urban, and a nation of country riflemen slowly turned into a nation of city dwellers. These urban citizens often turned to the pistol for self-defense. Cities eventually created police departments and armed them with pistols. The Federal Bureau of Investigation was instituted and also armed its agents. In 1911, the United States military adopted a semiautomatic pistol, the famous Colt 1911. And of course, the do-gooders hadn't yet decided that the public could not be trusted, so private citizens also kept pistols handy for defense against ruffians and scofflaws.

Early handgunning methods were not much different from what was common in the Old West. Contrary to western lore, few Old West pistoleros were good shots. Use of the sights was not widely practiced, and hit rates were not much better than what we see today from minimally trained personnel. What they did have going for them was the fact that they had no hesitation or remorse about killing, often walking up to fist-fighting distance and shooting their adversaries by surprise.

With few exceptions, the state of the art remained pretty much unchanged until just prior to World War II, when a great deal of research on gunfighting was done by men like British army officer W.E. Fairbairn. Fairbairn was one of those rare men who could kill an adversary in the afternoon and then study the dynamics of the fight and describe in detail at the evening meal why he won and the other fellow lost.

Fairbairn passed on much of his information to Col. Rex Applegate of the U.S. Army. The resulting school of thought, in essence and theory, focused on a man's likely reactions during a surprise close-range gunfight. The technique these men developed involved one-handed pointing of the pistol, with a fully extended arm, from a crouching position. This worked fairly well at close quarters but not as well at other times.

In the late 1950s and early 1960s, a curious group called the Bear Valley Gunslingers, headed by retired U.S. Marine Col. Jeff Cooper, began holding unrestricted shooting competitions, which eventually gave rise to the International Practical Shooting Confederation (IPSC). Cooper's "Modern Technique," which was a conglomeration of various concepts that he'd seen work best in those competitions, called for using both hands on the pistol with an isometric grip and acquiring a "flash sight picture."

Cooper's Modern Technique went beyond the competitive realm and became widely accepted as the most versatile

The rest has been due to the high level of skill sought by today's operators as well as the proliferation of quality shooting institutions.

method for pistol employment. It was just as quick as the previous methods for close quarters shooting but much more accurate beyond arm's length. Techniques which are, in essence, derivatives of Cooper's two-handed methods are still considered the most useful today.

CHAPTER 2

THE ULTIMATE
SERVICE PISTOL

When selecting a fighting pistol, there are certain guidelines that you should keep in mind. Primarily, a good handgun is selected for ease of carry and concealability. This doesn't mean that the smallest gun is the best but simply that the weapon must be of reasonable size and weight given its intended mission. With few exceptions, the role of the handgun in the tactical big picture is to allow the operator to regain control of his environment when unexpectedly faced with a threat. You will need to have access to it quickly and easily, so it must be comfortable to have around.

The chosen size of the handgun is often limited by the individual's lifestyle. A stockbroker living in New York, for example, could not expect to carry a 6-inch revolver in his daily attire, but a rancher in the Southwest would have no problem doing so.

Anyone who even casually peruses the pages of gun magazines is bombarded with stories and opinions about what is the best gun for self-defense. The opinions are as varied as the writers. A popular notion is that most service pistols need extensive reworking in order to make them combat worthy. In fact, an entire industry has developed around the perceived need to make out-of-the-box-stock pistols into "real" combat

The American "ultimate service pistol," the .45 auto. This one is from Caspian Arms. (Photo courtesy of Chuck Taylor.)

weapons. This idea has created a virtual subcategory of shooter who does nothing but customize and modify his handgun. For these folks, firearms are not weapons any longer but art objects.

But is such extravagance really necessary or even desirable? No doubt some degree of modification may enhance the combative utility of a handgun, but how much do you need? What advantage will a beautiful, museum-quality pistol provide you when you must use it to kill an assailant? When questioned by officials after the incident, how will you explain all the bells, whistles, and your name engraved on the polished nickel-plated slide?

My colleagues and I have studied the actual requirements for a combat-ready pistol from a real-world perspective. Many of us are still "in the business" and have had to shoot for blood on several occasions. Therefore, we take the subject of what is necessary to win a fight very seriously.

I conferred at length with these gentlemen on the desired attributes of a combat pistol and arrived at a set of requirements for what we would consider the best and most efficient defensive tool available today, the "ultimate" service pistol.

The primary requirement is that the pistol operates reliably. The fully loaded pistol must fire every time the operator presses the trigger. There is no compromise to be made here. Reliability takes precedence over intrinsic accuracy, ergonomics, or anything else. Given modern manufacturing methods for both firearms and cartridges, 100 percent reliability is *not* out of the question.

The ideal service pistol must allow the operator to place his shots on target accurately. Its design and characteristics must not impede this in any way. Just how much accuracy is needed? The weapon must have the inherent capability to place controlled shots on the chest of a man at 50 meters or in the cranial-ocular cavity at conversational distances. Nothing less will do. The other edge of the blade is that we need *not* have the ability to place the shots neatly on the third button of his shirt at such distances. This is especially the case if "accurizing" adversely affects reliability.

The defensive pistol must be powerful enough to end the hostilities with the minimum number of shots fired. Gunfights tend to be high-intensity, short-duration events. Rarely will anyone have time to fire more than a handful of shots. With that in mind, those shots must be as powerful as the operator can control. For some, this might mean that they could carry a .45 ACP. For others, a sure hit with a 9mm beats a tenuous miss with a .45. A good compromise is the relatively new .40 S&W (most other calibers being at least 50 years old). The rule of thumb: carry the biggest caliber that you can realistically control under high-stress tactical conditions.

The fighting pistol must be easy to use. Any structural impediments to rapid deployment are to be avoided. For

*The Italian "ultimate service pistol,"
a Beretta Model 92F.*

example, the pistol must be free of sharp edges. These days, a pistol is often carried concealed, which means that it spends a lot of time next to the operator's skin. Any sharp edges or ungainly designs will be felt immediately, causing the person to hastily choose an alternate weapon or, worse yet, leave the pistol at home!

Given the environments in which a service pistol will be carried, a rugged corrosion-resistant finish is important. I prefer a dark matte finish on mine. To me, a light-colored gun is a liability because it reflects every bit of available light. Even so-called matte finishes reflect light. (Hold a matte hard-chromed gun against a black T-shirt and you will instantly see what I mean.) There are others who disagree with me on this and prefer one of the nickel or stainless finishes. To each his own, but the gun must be corrosion and wear resistant. The better finishes, such as Robar's NP3 or Roguard, will provide all the corrosion resistance needed in a variety of colors and shades.

To fulfill the reliability requirement, it is important to avoid excessive "accurizing." Listen carefully: any modern stock pistol of reputable manufacture, loaded with high-quality factory ammunition, has more intrinsic accuracy than any human being can utilize under stress.

To ensure maximum reliability, you must select a pistol that is in excellent working condition, load it with high-quality factory ammunition suitable for defensive purposes, and use high-quality magazines to feed it. Next, fire several hundred rounds of your chosen load to make sure your pistol functions reliably with it and that you can hit a man in the important places with it. Finally, inspect all of your equipment for any damage or wear after each training session. After you have done all of this, don't worry about accuracy or reliability anymore!

Some basic modifications can be made to a fighting pistol to enhance its capabilities. First, make sure it is free of sharp edges. You don't need to grind away every corner; simply sand off any sharp points. Run your hand over the gun and make note of questionable spots. After a couple of firing sessions and a little time carrying it concealed, you will know which edges must be removed.

A manageable trigger is also desirable. Does this mean you need a 3 ounce, high-maintenance trigger job that requires more attention than tropical fish? No! Granted, a Glock or Browning/1911 trigger is easier to operate than a double-action (DA) trigger, but I have seen some very fine shooting done with DAs. A double-action trigger is no impediment if the operator practices with it. Sometimes these triggers are in need of slight polishing to smooth out "grit," "creep," or other irregularities, but it is generally a minor thing. I have seen several DA-armed shooters do quite well at many of the combat courses I have attended and taught.

High-visibility sights are essential. This is one area where

The Austrian "ultimate service pistol," a Glock 22 in .40 S&W.

manufacturers have listened to the shooting public and responded accordingly. Virtually every defensive pistol of reputable make is now issued with such sights. For those who desire them, tritium-equipped night sights are a worthy addition to any fighting pistol, especially if the issued sights are fragile (as with Glocks).

"OK, OK, I understand and agree with your requirements for the ideal defensive pistol," you say. But you are not satisfied. You want to see a picture of it, maybe even a centerfold of the *ultimate service pistol* replete with two-tone finish and custom ivory stocks, with the morning-mist condensation beading ever so slightly on the polished mirror finish of the slide as it lies suggestively on the freshly shot center of an IPSC target. Mouth-watering, isn't it?

The Ultimate Service Pistol

Well, I have never seen such a pistol in service with experienced operators. The guns of the men who really use them are nothing fancy or pretty; just simple, basic, reliable equipment. None of these pistols will ever be seen on the cover of *Playgun*, but then again, none of them will cost you very much either. Certainly they will not approach the cost of a Super Duper Hostage Rescue CQB Advanced Signature Model, but you can take the balance of the money you saved and spend it on several cases of ammunition to practice with and to carry in your sidearm. You can even use some of your savings to get some training in how to use your simple, basic, reliable equipment from those who have really "been there, done that" . . . and who still do.

When a good shooter with a poor gun meets a poor shooter with a good gun, the good shooter will have the good gun. Think about it, and get your perspective back on track. You can spend thousands of your dollars and hours of your precious time acquiring a delectable artifact that is beautiful to look at and photograph, or you can get a solid fighting tool and spend your money and time learning how to use it. If you choose the latter path—the warrior's path—then you will have realized, as my colleagues and I have, that it is the man and not the gun that makes the difference. If you take nothing else from this book, remember that!

CHAPTER 3

AMMUNITION SELECTION AND BALLISTICS

As important as selection of the pistol is the choice of ammunition to carry in it. That ammunition, after all, is what you are actually staking your life on. This is a critical and complex issue. It is critical because of what's at stake, and complex because the adversary, a human being, is amazingly resilient to damage.

In almost every gun magazine, some scribe foists upon the readership the new-improved answer to the ammunition question. Many people have made fortunes by selling "magic" bullets. The problem is that it's not nearly as simple as they make it out to be ("one-shot stops" and all of that sort of *basura*!). We must therefore examine some realities when choosing a cartridge on which we are going to bet everything.

Shot placement is one of the most important issues to consider. A miss with a 20mm cannon will not do what a .22 Short in the eye will. Given the expectation of suitable combat accuracy, the actual choice of caliber becomes equally important.

Shooting incidents are often sudden, high-intensity, short-duration events characterized by rapid and unpredictable movement, limited windows of opportunity, poor light, and confused communications. Such circumstances often lead to the shooter hitting the easiest target, which is simply the center of mass, or more specifically the center of whatever target area on the adversary is available. A study of police shootings reveals that regardless of the number of rounds fired, most of the time only one to three shots can actually be expected to hit the adversary. With this in mind, we must choose a round that will do the most amount of damage with the least number of rounds needed to inflict that damage, thereby increasing the likelihood of immediate incapacitation.

The mechanisms of wounding from a pistol bullet include penetration, permanent cavity, temporary cavity, and fragmentation and/or expansion.

The fragmentation or expansion properties of a pistol bullet are highly variable, and one must be careful to avoid betting everything on this. Expansion and fragmentation from rifle bullets that travel in excess of 2000 feet per second is one thing. It is an entirely different matter when it relates to relatively slow-moving pistol bullets. The fastest of pistol bullets cannot travel fast enough to guarantee expansion without fail in a human adversary; there are just too many variables present. Even with custom, specially designed "manstoppers," there will always be one that will not perform as advertised. If that one happens to be yours, hope you live to get your money back!

The temporary cavity formed by the displacement of tissue, temporarily, by the forces entering the body vis a vis the bullet is not an important incapacitation mechanism because the cavity is simply too small. Preeminent medical professionals and expert ballisticians of the International Wound Ballistics Association opine that elastic tissues may be displaced as much as 4 inches without serious discomfort, much less incapacitation. Again, temporary cavitation is certainly an issue with rifle calibers, but not pistol calibers.

The only reliable mechanisms for incapacitation from a pistol-caliber bullet are penetration to the vital organs and the tissue which is physically destroyed as a result of that penetration (i.e., the permanent cavity). Most knowledgeable persons in the study of wound trauma believe that adequate penetration depth is by far the most important consideration in the selection of pistol ammunition. The minimum depth has been assumed to be 12 inches, but 14 or even 16 inches may be better given the potential to have to shoot through intermediate barriers such as arm muscles, heavy clothing, or light cover.

After penetration, the most essential element of incapacitation is the size of the hole the bullet produces via that penetration. Penetration is a function of sectional density and velocity. Sectional density is a function of cross-sectional area as well as weight. The bottom line is that the heaviest bullet available, in the largest caliber you can handle, is the ticket. Certain bullet designs may offer the potential for enhanced damage via expansion at the outer limits of penetration. This is a bonus, but don't go the expansion route at the sacrifice of penetration.

With respect to bullet weight, in .45 ACP, any 230-grain round should be the top choice. In .40 S&W the 180 grain is my preference, and in 9mm, the 147 grain would get the vote. Federal, Speer, Remington, Hornady, or Winchester offerings in any of these calibers are good choices. The Black Talon (recently renamed SXT), Golden Saber, Gold Dot, or Hydra-Shok are all good, combat-proven choices that may provide additional benefits from expansion. Avoid rounds that are unproven or that, when fired, are uncontrollable. Also to be avoided are rounds that rely excessively on their velocity to be effective. This velocity is often a trade-off for lighter bullets, which will penetrate less and exhibit excessive muzzle flash when fired.

The bottom line is to choose ammunition that has been used successfully in combat and that is manufactured by an established company. Select the heaviest, moderate-velocity round available. Make certain that the round shoots and functions well in your weapon . . . and then be prepared for the time when you hit your adversary and he doesn't go down.

CHAPTER 4

NECESSARY ACCESSORIES

Selection of the handgun and ammunition is not the end of the story. To use this tool to its greatest level, you need a few more things. Unless the extent of your handgunning activities will be presenting the weapon from a desk drawer or nightstand, you need a holster, a belt that matches that holster, and a pouch to carry at least one spare magazine for the pistol.

In my opinion, a handgun without a holster is like a sword without a sheath. Fortunately, there are more holster designs today than there are pistol designs. That's good for the consumer because of the variety of products to choose from, but it is also a point of concern because the unknowing might make a bad decision on a purchase. In this case, a bad purchase may cost you your life! Serious consideration of the issue becomes mandatory for anyone who intends to carry the weapon for tactical/defensive purposes, regardless of whether he is a police officer, private citizen, or military operator.

The purposes of a holster are several. First, it is a carrying apparatus for the firearm. It must keep the weapon in a fixed position at all times. Otherwise, it becomes difficult to quickly obtain, gain control of, and bring the pistol into action. Therefore one of the important characteristics of a sound hol-

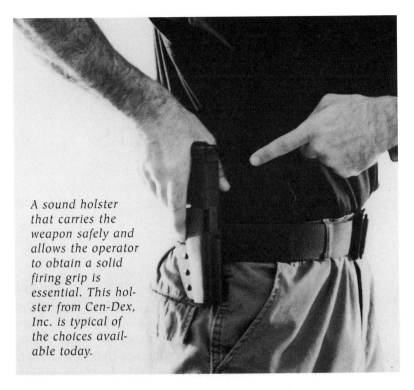

A sound holster that carries the weapon safely and allows the operator to obtain a solid firing grip is essential. This holster from Cen-Dex, Inc. is typical of the choices available today.

ster must be belt loops that are sufficiently wide to allow a certain amount of rigidity on the belt.

Second, the holster must secure the weapon from loss. Certainly the pistol will do you no good if it's not there because it fell out of its holster as you exited your car!

Third, the holster must protect the weapon in the environment in which it will be carried. Although dust, moisture, and impact damage are all things to be considered, common sense must be exercised by selecting a holster that is appropriate for the situation. A man carrying a pistol in the murky jungles of a Third World hot spot does not have the same requirements as a police detective assigned to a desk in New York.

Finally, the holster must provide the fastest possible acquisition and presentation. When you need a pistol, you probably need it really bad. Most pistol fights take place just outside of arm's length, meaning that engagements are quick and intense. A holster that demands preplanning to get the weapon out is *not* a good choice.

Selecting a holster that fulfills all those requirements is not easy. Primarily, you must define your particular circumstances. We all have different life-styles and requirements. As such, there is no such thing as a "universal holster" (although I'll bet someone will try to sell you one). The top choice of a police detective will likely not be the choice of an operator on an antiterrorist team. Nor will the choice of a duty policeman be the choice of the private citizen with a CCW permit.

Regardless of the holster chosen, it *must* exhibit two basic characteristics: it must allow the wearer to obtain a firing grip on the pistol while it is still holstered, and it must cover enough of the trigger guard area to prevent unintentional access to the trigger by the trigger finger or other objects such as clothing or twigs. This will help eliminate unintentional discharges.

Weapon security is certainly a concern, but it must be balanced against speed of presentation. Far too many police holsters are slanted so much on the side of security that a speedy presentation is not even a consideration. Again, a balance must be established that provides a degree of security against disarming but allows the pistol to be presented quickly enough to make a difference in a sudden confrontation. In this case, a simple thumb-break design will often suffice. Many holsters offer a secondary retention device or design. If it does not impair the presentation, then it is a welcome addition.

Materials used for holster designs today range from simple leather to high-tech plastics. I seriously recommend one made from Kydex or Concealex. These new materials are state-of-the-art thermo-plastics, which are form-fit to the pistol. They provide an actual snap-fit to secure the weapon while still allowing an extremely fast presentation. Many big-name holster companies now offer these holsters as stock items, whereas they were once a custom proposition only.

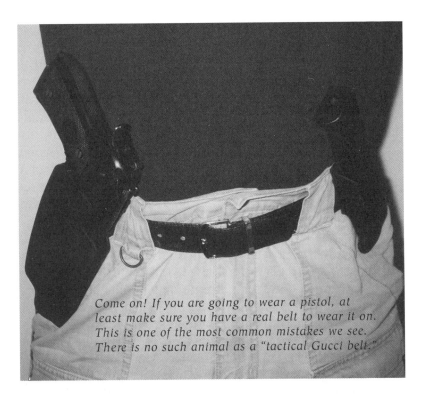

Come on! If you are going to wear a pistol, at least make sure you have a real belt to wear it on. This is one of the most common mistakes we see. There is no such animal as a "tactical Gucci belt."

They are available from such manufacturers such as High Desert Holsters, Blade-Tech, and Sidearmor (all of which can be located on the Internet). Many of these designs are just as popular with private citizens as with police officers and military personnel.

Almost as important as the holster is the carry method for additional magazines. Everything we've said about holsters also applies to extra magazine pouches. Fortunately, these pouches are usually available from the same sources as the holsters and in the same rugged materials.

The best holster and magazine pouch are next to useless if you do not place them on the appropriate belt. Specifically, the belt's width must match the holster and magazine pouch belt loops. Keep in mind the environments where you will be

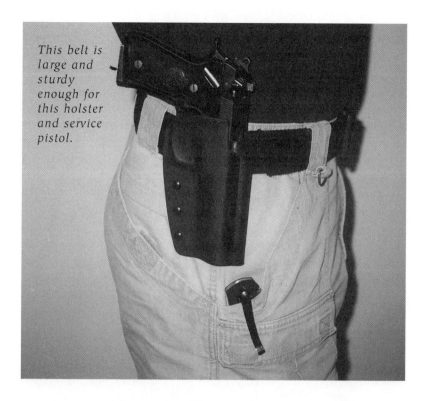

This belt is large and sturdy enough for this holster and service pistol.

wearing your sidearm as well as the dress code at those times. You cannot press a dress belt into service to carry a pistol; instead, you must purchase a special-purpose belt at least 1 1/4 inch in width so it fits the loops on a pair of fashionable European-cut business suit slacks as well as the loops of your holster. If you cannot find one of these, you may need to order a specific holster designed for a narrow belt.

I suggest avoiding the shoulder holster. It is not conducive to quick weapon presentations and, due to the fact that it places the muzzle of the weapon pointing toward everyone behind you, it is very difficult to train with. Moreover, it is difficult to maintain control of the holstered pistol during any violent activity such as the fisticuffs, which often precede gunfights. You gain nothing from such an

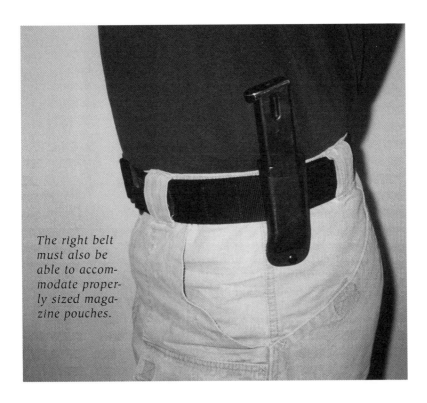

The right belt must also be able to accommodate properly sized magazine pouches.

arrangement that you cannot have from a standard belt holster and pouch configuration.

Quite popular these days is the "belly bag" carry mode. Many manufacturers produce a version of this rig. It allows the carry of a full-size weapon even when wearing the skimpiest of garments. I usually reserve mine for two situations: working out at the weight room (I do live in L.A., and, well, you never know) and when my sidearm is placed by the bedside. Packed with a few spare magazines, a tactical flashlight, a small fighting knife, a cell-phone, and a few other goodies, in an unexpected nocturnal emergency I can grab the bag and have all I need to go to war. Be advised that the ability to obtain a firing grip while holstered as well as coverage of the trigger guard are still essential.

Necessary Accessories

As you can see, holster selection demands more than simply grabbing anything the sales clerk offers you. Select this ancillary equipment as carefully as you select the pistol itself.

CHAPTER 5

PERFECT PRACTICE

Now that we have our hardware sorted out, let's discuss the actual issues of getting so good with it that you'll scare yourself. How good is "good enough"? That is a question that tactical shooters have been asking themselves and others since the days of flint and steel. And it is as easily answered today as it was in the past. When it comes to the issue of life and death, you can *never* be good enough!

The question is then slightly modified: just how good can you get? Only you can answer that, but this chapter will help you find out.

Perfect practice will help you hit your target—whether paper or flesh and blood—every time, on demand. This ability to hit is the very foundation of tactical shooting. All the high-speed, low-drag tactics in the world and all the Walter Mitty gear available will not save you if you cannot hit before you are hit.

Tactical shooting is a psychomotor, pseudoathletic skill. As such, shooting successfully (that means getting hits, Grasshopper!) depends partially on the "physical memorization" of the specific movements and their proper sequence. Perfecting the execution of these movements in sequence is best accomplished with extensive repetition that reinforces

It's not just about making a mountain of brass at the shooting range; it's about programming perfect reflexes through extensive and repetitive exercise. Dry practice is an essential part of this process, and you cannot become good without it!

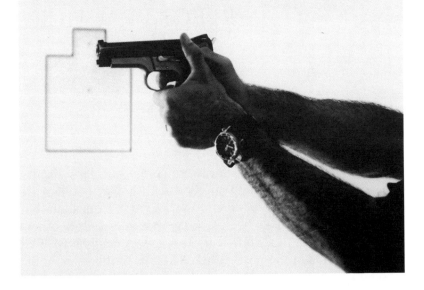

the neuromuscular programming required to execute them. The stronger this programming becomes, the more reflexive and subconscious the correct execution of the technique becomes. Most importantly when dealing with intense real-world confrontations, the stronger this programming becomes, the less conscious thought will be required to perform the neurologically ingrained techniques.

This concept of physical memorization and subconscious programming is not new. In the 1600s, the Japanese sword master Yagyu Tajima No Kami wrote, "Learning and knowledge are meant to be forgotten, and it is only when this is realized, that you feel perfectly comfortable. The body will move as if automatically, without conscious effort on the part of the swordsman himself. All of the training is there, but the mind is utterly unconscious of it." Yagyu was, of course, writing about swordsmanship, but the concept is just as valid for combat marksmanship.

Physiologists have determined that it takes nearly 3,000 repetitions for a technique or skill to become a conditioned reflex. And make no mistake, dear reader: in a confrontation where your life is measured in heartbeats and you have little time to think, conditioned reflexes are exactly what you must have!

But be careful! You do not want to simply do 3,000 repetitions. You must achieve 3000 *perfect* repetitions. Even one substandard repetition tends to sabotage the entire process and may even program imperfect reactions. It is just as important for a world-class baseball pitcher to throw 3,000 perfect pitches as it is for a golfer to swing 3,000 perfect strokes. Certainly no one would argue that this is even more the case for the tactical shooter, whose stakes far exceed those of any mere sport.

A tactical shooter—whether private citizen, police officer, or professional soldier—literally bets his life on his skill in a confrontation. When he faces his grim adversary in a greasy alley, in some God-forsaken desert wadi, or in his own living room at zero dark thirty, he has no one to help him and nothing to rely on but his warrior's attitude, his sidearm, and his perfectly programmed fighting responses.

Following the procedures described in this book will help you not only establish but also polish the skills needed to stand tall when the chips are down. And a major portion of your success in this endeavor will come from a serious program of dry-fire practice.

There is a story about a man named Dave Westerhout who spent considerable time in the Rhodesian Defense Force. The political sanctions imposed on his country caused an extreme shortage of practice ammunition. Rather than make do with the paltry ration of training ammunition, he attempted to determine if troops could be trained to a reasonable level of proficiency without ever firing their weapons until qualification day. The result of Westerhout's experiments was that the group he trained, using dry practice only, shot slightly higher scores than the group that had been trained in the conventional live-fire method.

Dry practice is the effort a student puts forth off the range, at home, with an *unloaded* pistol. It is an essential method for developing and polishing skills because it allows you to execute perfect repetitions without the distractions of muzzle blast or recoil.

The reason for this is simple. The mechanics of shooting are a motor reflex. Motor reflexes are enhanced with repetition. Dry practice allows you to execute a vast number of perfect repetitions.

Many so-called experts eschew dry practice altogether and instead advocate prodigious amounts of ammunition expenditure in live-fire drills. This is a horrible mistake. I have found that the more you shoot, the worse shot you become!

Live fire is an important but minor part of the overall training of a tactical shooter. Each shot that is fired imprints subconscious programming into the nervous system. This is fine if the shot is fired with perfect concentration and control. But a problem arises because you cannot maintain perfect concentration indefinitely. Some can manage perfect concentration for only a few shots. Even highly trained expert shooters cannot concentrate fully for more than 100 shots at any one session. Any monkey can be trained to "mash" the trigger, fire uncontrolled shots, and accomplish nothing but making brass. A man who wants to be better strives for a perfect shot *every time* he presses the trigger. Every imperfect shot programs the subconscious improperly.

Given this, live-fire practice must become a simple validation of your dry-practice training and programming, not the sole focus of your training. Think of dry practice as the training and live fire as the final exam which insures that your training is right. If you find yourself shooting poorly, you do not need more shooting! Quite to the contrary, you need more dry practice.

Dry practice will allow you to perfect every action associated with the act of firing a shot and therefore will do more for you than shooting 10,000 rounds of ammunition. But I am not suggesting that dry practice entirely replace live-fire training. Nor do I discourage you from seeking out professional firearms and tactical training. Both of these activities are essential to full skill development.

You must obtain professional instruction from men with actual combat experience. Being exposed to such real-world perspective is an invaluable way to learn the hows and whys of tactical shooting. Additionally, you must fire live ammunition periodically in order to remind your subconscious mind what the actual discharge of a shot and recoil feel like. This way you will become a complete shooter. But dry practice will help you perfect the new skills you learn from the pros as well as help you program them into your subconscious mind. This, in turn, is guaranteed to improve your shooting.

I've included brief but descriptive chapters on the basics of gun handling that build upon what I covered in *The Tactical Pistol*. Study them and get the proper procedures down. I also strongly recommend reading the books listed in Appendix C as well as seeking professional training. This will give you a complete overview on the matter. When you have a good understanding of the topic and have memorized the proper procedures, especially the dry-practice safety guidelines outlined in the next chapter, you may begin programming the skills into your subconscious mind through dry-practice training.

The first objective of dry practice is to program the mechanics and basics of tactical shooting into your muscle memory. Do not omit this part, even if you consider yourself an accomplished shooter. This basic gun-handling training may point out mistakes or bad habits that we all acquire through the years. If you do not find these "minor" errors, you will simply be reinforcing them when you practice. This is certainly not the goal of a program entitled "perfect."

Eventually you will move on to executing the techniques within specified time intervals. Don't get carried away with trying to beat the clock here. The time interval exists only to provide a degree of urgency to the drill as well as to give you an idea of your level of skill in relation to standard time limits. Practice the basic routine until you are performing with certain smoothness. Then strive to be smooth under the time limit. Success comes from performing correct procedures fluidly.

Now, place the dry-practice target (included in this book as Appendix B) on a solid backing at eye level and verify again that you have followed all the safety procedures. You are taking an important step here, a step that will improve your shooting skills and, vicariously, your personal safety in an increasingly dangerous world.

CHAPTER 6

SAFETY AND SAFE DRY PRACTICE

Any discussion of firearm utilization must include a discussion of safety. This is especially the case with a book intended to be used for skill enhancement. So we take the inherent danger of firearms training into account and seek to establish rules and procedures by which to manage it.

The following safety rules are standard with all professional gun handlers and as important for the first-time gun buyer as for the SWAT or SpecOps expert.

RULE ONE—Treat all guns as if they are loaded. An unloaded gun, while comforting to the squeamish, is all but useless for self-defense. Their utility comes into play only when loaded. That is their natural condition, so always assume they are until you've proven otherwise by checking the chamber.

RULE TWO—Do not allow your muzzle to cover anything you are not willing to destroy. This is fairly self-explanatory and includes television sets as well as live adversaries.

Now, a word about actual armed confrontations. When facing a hostile adversary, you are quite justified in covering him with your weapon rather than holding it at the ready. Many authorities disagree with me on this, but the fact remains that if you have decided that you are in danger and are therefore willing to destroy an adversary, it is in no way a violation of safety to cover him with your muzzle until the situation is under control. But this leads to the next rule . . .

RULE THREE—Keep your finger OFF the trigger until you've made a conscious decision to shoot. Guns do not "go off" by themselves. Someone makes them go off, usually by pressing the trigger. This action may be intentional or the result of negligence. In any case, it cannot happen to you if you observe Rule Three.

To facilitate observance of this rule, I recommend that you locate an index point of sorts on the frame of your pistol. This point should be located naturally where the trigger finger lies on the frame when you are striving to keep it off the trigger. Make a point of always placing your finger on that point of reference. That way it will either be on the trigger when it is needed or on the index point on stand by.

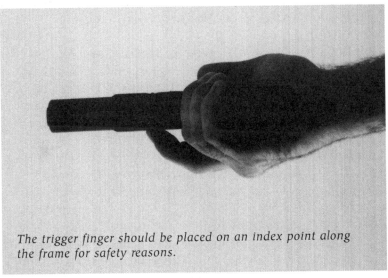

The trigger finger should be placed on an index point along the frame for safety reasons.

RULE FOUR—Be sure of your target and what is beyond it. Do not shoot at a sound or a shadow unless you are double damn sure of what it is. Sometimes shooting through doors or walls is necessary in SpecOps and SWAT environments, but this is rarely the case in a private citizen's defensive role. Remember—be dead sure about your target and what is behind it.

These four safety rules are applicable in a tactical situation as well as at the firing range or during dry practice. Make them a daily practice and point of focus and you will never have a problem with safe gun handling.

In terms of dry practice, there are some additional procedures that you must follow in order to prevent any mishaps.

1) Set a reasonable time limit for the dry practice session, certainly no more than 30 minutes at any one session. If your concentration begins to lapse, it is time to stop.

2) Designate a dry practice area. This will be your official dry practice area, and *all* dry practice will be done there. This area should have a sufficient backstop in the event that a shot is fired inadvertently.

3) Unload your weapon, all magazines, and all ammunition carriers. Chamber check the pistol after unloading to make sure.

4) Place *all* the ammunition in an area other than the dry practice area, such as in another room.

5) Place the dry practice target in such a manner that if a negligent discharge of the weapon were to occur, the bullet would be captured in the building material or travel in a direction that would not cause damage or injury.

6) Only display the dry practice target while practicing. As soon as the session is over, remove and store the target.

7) Present the weapon, point it in a safe direction, and recheck to make certain it is in fact unloaded (see chamber checking procedures in the next chapter). Double

check all magazines as well to be certain that there is *absolutely no live ammunition* on your person or in the dry practice area.

8) You are now ready to mentally enter the dry practice session. Concentrate on the dry practice drills described in Chapter 19. Avoid all distractions. If you experience any distractions such as a phone call, knock at the door, or whatever, stop the dry practice session immediately. If you decide to continue with the session after the distraction has been dealt with, go back to step one and proceed through the safety checks again.

9) After the dry practice is completed, you must mentally leave the session. Immediately remove and store the target, leave the dry practice area, and tell yourself out loud, "I have finished my dry practice session. Dry practice is over."

10) At this point, you may load your weapon or place it in its normal condition and review the four basic safety rules.

Some of you may think that this is a tedious bit of nit-picking on my part, but I assure you that it is necessary from both a liability and a safety perspective. More negligent discharges occur during routine gun handling and dry practice than at any other time. Every private citizen who has a negligent discharge is another exclamation point for the people in our society wishing to ban firearms.

But private citizens are not alone in their responsibility. Many shots are fired negligently in police locker rooms, for example. There is a nice .45 caliber hole in the locker next to mine at police headquarters that narrowly missed several officers by inches! It was fired by an extremely competent, but now retired, veteran police officer who was simply too tired to be bothered with basic safety precautions. There are other stories of officers and private citizens alike being shot unintentionally during routine gun handling. Save yourself a lot of grief, embarrassment, and quite possibly a tragedy and heed every word in this chapter.

CHAPTER 7

LOADING, UNLOADING, AND CHAMBER CHECKING

One often neglected aspect of gun handling is the status check, or "chamber check." Many people who handle weapons on a daily basis can become complacent about them. Familiarity breeds contempt, and this is quite true with regards to firearms. The following procedures will help prevent tragedies that arise from such complacency.

Conducting a chamber check in order to ascertain its condition *must* become a reflexive action every time you pick up a firearm. This is recommended during administrative gun handling as well as prior to entering a tactical situation (if you have the time, of course). My colleague Marc Fleischmann calls the chamber check "one second of cheap insurance." This is so true. Virtually all of the negligent discharges that I am aware of might have been avoided if the operator had verified the condition of his pistol with a quick check of the chamber. Additionally, if you know that you are probably going to get in a gunfight in the next few minutes, wouldn't you want to make double damn sure that your pistol was really loaded? I sure would. All it takes is one second.

At this point, I should mention some terminology that I will use throughout the book. Your primary hand is the hand you utilize to hold and fire the pistol; your support hand is the

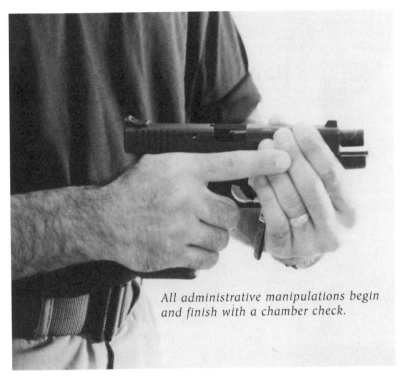

All administrative manipulations begin and finish with a chamber check.

other hand. Any body part (arm, foot, etc.) on the primary side is called primary, and similarly with the support side. The loading mechanism is called a magazine, not a "clip." A grip is what you do with your hand; the stocks (or frame on pistols that do not incorporate stocks) are the area of the pistol that you grab.

There are several established ways to check a chamber. The method you select will depend on the type of pistol you are armed with. When operating with a pistol that is equipped with slide-mounted decocking levers such as the Beretta 92, Smith & Wesson pistols, and similar models, use the following procedure.

Present the pistol to the ready position (see Chapter 10). Every time you present a pistol with decocking levers that also function as safety levers, you must physically make sure that the levers are disengaged. Condition yourself to execute the thrust of the primary thumb that disengages them, even if you carry them disengaged (just in case).

Bring the pistol inward toward your torso for more leverage and to be able to look down into the chamber area, but be careful to control the muzzle at all times. Lower the decocking levers and place your support index finger and middle finger, straddling the slide, on either side of the levers. Place your support thumb on the tang of the pistol. Now "pinch" the slide open about 1/4 inch to be able to visually inspect the chamber.

If you are equipped with a pistol that does not have the slide-mounted decocking levers, such as the Glock series, the Colt/Browning series, or the SIG Sauer, use the following method instead. Note that on the Colt/Browning pistols you must disengage the safety levers, as it is designed to be carried "cocked and locked." With the SIG Sauer, you must first manually cock the hammer because of the overly strong issue mainspring.

Present the pistol to the ready position. You may bring the pistol closer for leverage and increased visibility, but be careful about the direction of the muzzle. Bring the support hand over the top of the pistol, being careful to avoid the muzzle. Place the thumb on one side of the slide with the thumbprint touching the grooves located at the rear of the slide and the other fingers on the opposite side. Now move the slide to the rear approximately 1/4 inch and visually inspect the chamber.

If you cannot operate the slide as described above because of insufficient hand strength or because your pistol has a slippery finish, do not despair. Adapt and overcome, as the drill instructors were fond of saying! Grab the slide further to the rear on the serrated grasping grooves and then conduct the chamber check. Be careful that you do not actuate the slide too far because that will either chamber a round or eject a chambered round.

Whichever method you use, you may also incorporate a tactile round verification by simply using the primary hand trigger finger or the support hand index finger to feel for a chambered round.

A second part of the chamber check is to visually inspect the magazine. I know of several instances where chamber checks were conducted by police officers after a training session and then returned to duty . . . with empty magazines! Luckily no good guys got hurt, but you can well imagine the potential for disaster.

The chamber check should become an automatic action every single time you pick up your pistol in an administrative environment and prior to entering a tactical environment if there is time. It must also precede and follow all loading and unloading procedures.

The loading procedure for any autoloading pistol begins at the ready position with a chamber check. Verifying that the pistol is unloaded, insert a loaded magazine into the pistol. Maintaining the pistol in the ready position, grasp the grooves located at the rear of the slide with the support hand. Pull the slide to the rear briskly. When the slide reaches its rearmost position, allow it to move forward from the power of the recoil spring. Do not "ride" the slide forward with the support hand. Instead, let go of the slide and allow the rearward motion of the support hand to continue until it reaches the firing side shoulder. Resume the two-handed grip in the ready position. You have just chambered a round, but you must make sure by conducting a final chamber check, including a magazine check. That concludes the loading procedure in administrative situations. Just remember: during an actual confrontation you may not have time to check the gun's status, but always do so if there is time.

Obtain and insert a magazine into the pistol in the same manner as you would in an emergency.

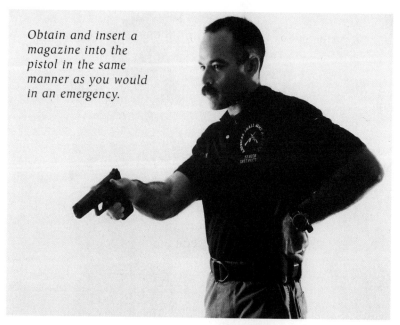

Insert the magazine.

Seat the magazine.

Cycle the slide.

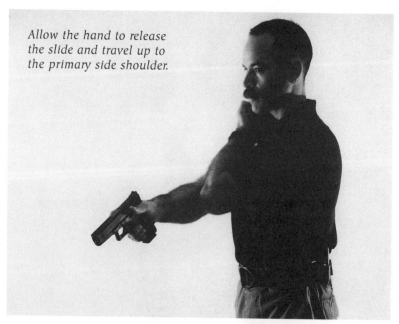

Allow the hand to release the slide and travel up to the primary side shoulder.

Re-acquire a two-handed grip on the pistol.

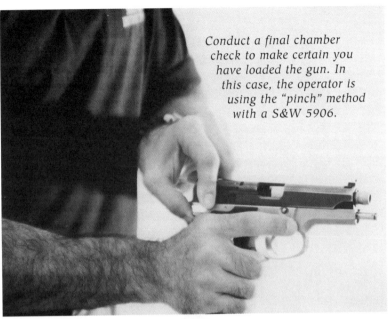

Conduct a final chamber check to make certain you have loaded the gun. In this case, the operator is using the "pinch" method with a S&W 5906.

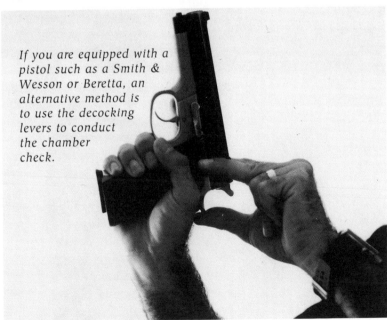

If you are equipped with a pistol such as a Smith & Wesson or Beretta, an alternative method is to use the decocking levers to conduct the chamber check.

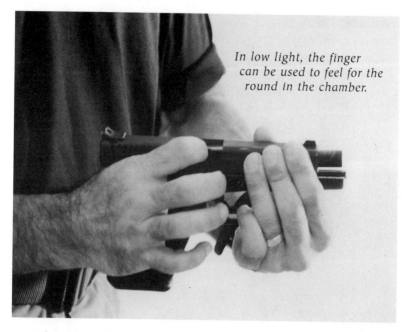

In low light, the finger can be used to feel for the round in the chamber.

The unloading procedure also begins with the pistol in the ready position. The first thing to do is conduct a chamber check. The sequence of events is very important. First, remove the magazine and place it between the little finger and ring finger of the primary hand. This way you know exactly where that magazine is, and you are certain that you have removed it. Next, place your support hand over the ejection port so that your hand is cupping it. Turn the pistol 90 degrees outboard so that the ejection port is facing down. Cycle the slide to the rear slowly, allowing the chambered round to fall into your support hand. Place that round in your pocket, place that magazine in your pocket, and re-acquire the two-handed hold in the ready position. You have now unloaded your pistol, but make sure with a final chamber check.

Some schools favor dropping the chambered round on the ground when unloading. I avoid this for a number of reasons. It is not so much an issue with training ammo, but remember that your carry ammo also gets cycled in the load-unload process. Any carry round that lands on the deck should be taken out of service. For those who think I'm being picky about this, understand that every time a round hits the ground the rim may get slightly damaged, as may the bullet itself. All these things may affect its performance. That round in the chamber, right now, may be the one you'll need to save your life. Treat it accordingly.

Remember that perfect gun handling is intended not only to get hits on target quickly and efficiently but also to prevent negligent, unintentional, or accidental shots from being fired. Programming the chamber check procedure as well as the loading and unloading procedures into your memory will go far in keeping you and yours safe during "routine" gun handling.

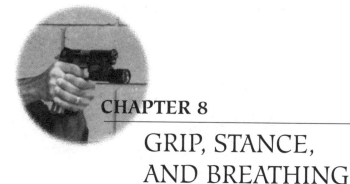

CHAPTER 8

GRIP, STANCE, AND BREATHING

To repeat an earlier clarification, a grip is what your hand does to the pistol. The area that you grasp is called the stocks (or frame in the case of Glock pistols). So when I talk about grip, I mean your physical hold on the pistol.

The grip serves only one purpose: to hold the pistol in place while you operate the trigger. It must not in any way impede your placing accurate shots on target. This includes holding it too tightly.

The best grip allows the pistol to sit extremely low in the hand, with the tang deep in the web of the hand. The lower the pistol sits in the hand, the more control you will be able to exert on it. The remainder of the fingers simply grab around the front of the pistol's frame, as high against the trigger guard as is comfortable. The primary thumb is held high along the top of the frame. This grip allows the trigger finger to operate carefully and under control. If you bear down with the thumb, not only do you risk accidentally pressing the magazine release button but you also deprive the trigger finger of much needed dexterity.

Grip the pistol as high up on the tang area as possible. There should not be any gap between the tang and the web of the hand, as shown here.

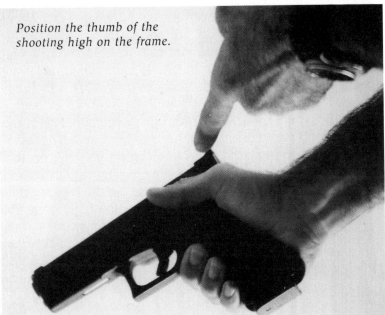

Position the thumb of the shooting high on the frame.

A low thumb may accidentally activate the magazine release button, preventing more than a single shot from being fired at all.

The support hand grips around the front of the primary hand. The support hand thumb takes a position alongside the primary hand thumb. An alternate but just as useful position for the support thumb is to place it in front of the primary thumb and actually rest the primary thumb on top of the support thumb. Either one will do. You will notice that both thumbs are held high and are otherwise uninvolved in anything else except staying out of the way. If the weapon is equipped with frame-mounted safety levers, such as the 1911 series, it's important to place the primary thumb on the safety lever anytime the pistol is in hand.

The grip itself is not a "death grip." Grasp the pistol about as hard as you would a friend's hand when greeting him. Many people make the mistake of over-gripping in an attempt to control the recoil. You cannot prevent the pistol from recoiling by exerting excessive pressure with your hands. You will, however, prevent proper trigger control with such a grip. A good index to use is this: if you see your front sight shaking

The fingers of the support hand should fit into the grooves created by the grip of the primary hand.

Both hands come together to envelop the frame area of the pistol and hold it in place during firing. The support thumb may be kept high . . .

*. . . or it may be placed forward on
the frame. I prefer the latter method.*

One of the most popular stances in modern times is the isosceles.

on target, you are holding too tight. Back it off to about 75 percent of that and you will have the right grip index.

The stance you use is not crucial as long as it provides certain things to the firing platform. I am well aware that a multitude of accomplished shooters favor the isosceles stance and think Weaver shooters are throwbacks. An equal number of accomplished folks believe anyone not shooting from a Weaver stance is an infidel. Some of them are very talented individuals who can probably shoot better in a competition with one hand and their eyes closed than the majority of shooters using two hands.

For many years I was a firm and exclusive proponent of the Weaver stance. I still favor and use the Weaver because it fits my body type. But I have also seen and trained with many shooters who are just as good firing from other stances. I've come to the conclusion that whatever stance you use or whatever you call it is not as important as making sure that it allows you to do the following.

A firing stance must provide a solid and stable platform from the waist up from which to fire the shots. How the feet are positioned is really not as important. It must also allow you to move, because when someone is trying to kill you and you are trying to do the same to him, you *will* move. You must have balance, and you must be able to maintain an aggressive posture. Whether you use a Weaver or isosceles is really irrelevant as long as you can be aggressive, balanced, and stable from the waist up.

When the mass of the firearm is above both arms, in what direction will the weapon move when it recoils? That's right, straight up! When you remember that it is desirable to always shoot an assailant twice (sometimes you must hit him twice a number of times!), this means that you will have some recovery time between shots. The speed with which those two shots are placed in the adversary is of critical importance because we are racing his nervous system to shut down. This is paramount to incapacitation.

Another very popular position is the Weaver.

Your upper body mass and weight is what contributes most to the management of recoil, not the positioning of the arms. An aggressive stance (i.e., leaning in) will allow the mass of your upper body to support the pistol's movement during the firing cycle, thereby lessening felt recoil and muzzle flip. In this way, the entire upper body, and not just the arms, controls the pistol.

While aggressiveness in a stance is important, don't go too far here. You cannot eliminate the weapon's recoil simply by leaning in. What you should specifically avoid is the straight or backward leaning stance of the bull's-eye or competitive shooter.

To assume a proper shooting/fighting stance (isosceles or Weaver), stand slightly bladed to the target, at about a 30 degree angle, with the support side foot leading by about half a step. Do not exaggerate the angle. Turning too much will create tension in the shoulder area, which in turn will cause lateral stringing of your shots. If you are not certain, measure out 30 degrees so you know what it feels like to stand that way!

Traditional isosceles shooters will notice that standing straight on to the target with feet side-by-side is de-emphasized in favor of a slightly bladed, one foot forward attitude. There are various tactical and physiological reasons for selecting a bladed posture instead of standing straight on. It provides greater balance for violent quick movements, you are able to keep the weapon side away from an adversary with the support side foot forward, and you will generally be in some variation of this posture when approached by a suspicious party (police call it the "interview position"). There are other reasons. For now, remember that we are cultivating a fighting posture, not just a shooting posture. Fighting and shooting are the same.

Keep the feet, knees, hips, and shoulder in line, without any twisting of the torso. Holding the pistol in a two-handed grip, extend it out toward the target. Keep the firing arm relatively straight, although it need not be locked. Bend the support side arm slightly. This is different than the two locked arms of the traditional isosceles, but it is a vast improvement because it is more natural as a fighting posture than an artificial "shooting stance."

For those who prefer a Weaver-oriented stance, bend the support side elbow so that it is pointing downward toward the ground. This in turn will create a slight isometric pressure, which will not only aid in getting indexed on target but will drastically reduce muzzle flip. Note that the isometric pressure is not a tensing of the muscles—you do not intentionally "push and pull." Proper pressure occurs naturally because of the configuration of the arms. Do not think push-pull; rather, simply get into a proper stance. Everything else will take care of itself. Bring the primary arm and the pistol up to the line of sight, without dipping the head to meet it. The rest involves the principles of marksmanship discussed in the next chapter.

The final point of discussion is breathing. I've saved it for last because in the intervals where most gunfighting takes place, breathing patterns are not a very serious issue. The main thing to remember about breathing is to keep doing it. This is not a joke. Under dynamic stress, I've found that many shooters actually hold their breath. This will not lead to anything desirable, and eventually you will get light-headed and may pass out. You will most likely hold your breath while you are actually pressing the trigger, but as you lower the pistol to low ready, b-r-e-a-t-h-e. The keys to remember are scan and breathe, scan and breathe.

There are situations where you will want finite surgical accuracy, including trying to make extremely long shots or hit extremely small target areas (e.g., emergency shots past innocent parties). In these circumstances, we borrow a page from the snipers and develop the respiratory pause. Inhale a lung full of air and exhale it. This does two things: it oxygenates the blood, giving you an eight second window before you must breathe again, and it relaxes your muscles so that the tension does not interfere with your marksmanship. As you exhale, you must begin the front sight focus and pressure on the trigger. Ideally, the shot will be discharged before you need to breathe again. This allows for extreme accuracy and is best executed from some sort of supported position, although a standing position will do fine if that's all you can do.

Never forget: the intent here is not learning to shoot handguns in the controlled environment of the firing range to hit bull's-eyes or win a medal. These are fine pursuits for those whose interest lies in those areas, but it is not the focus of this study. Rather, our purpose is to learn a life-saving skill with whatever pistol you happen to have on hand, loaded with realistic antipersonnel ammunition. For a further discussion of the fine points of grips and shooting stances, see my other book on handgunning, *The Tactical Pistol*.

CHAPTER 9

THE BASICS OF MARKSMANSHIP

Getting hits on a target is easy to do once you know how to do it. Like any other control- and dexterity-dependent skill, there is a proven and correct way to shoot a pistol.

I am not talking about bull's-eye shooting, although some of the skill involved in that discipline also corresponds to tactical shooting. We are primarily interested in self-defense shooting. This means that we want the ability to place solid hits on an adversary from a condition of unreadiness under urgent time limits.

Before you can expect to hit anything, some hardware issues must be addressed. First, your ammunition must be capable of an acceptable level of accuracy. This is not as much of a concern when using quality defensive ammunition, but it is when using more economical training ammo. Second, you must make certain that the pistol is zeroed correctly. This simply means that the sights must be arranged in a way that they will coincide visually with the physical impact of the bullet on target. There are hundreds of different types of sights, and to explain how to zero every particular weapon would take its own book. For zeroing procedures, refer to your weapon's training or owner's manual. Don't dismiss this part of the equation; doing so will only lead to frustration.

There are several fundamentals to marksmanship, includ-

Proper sight alignment, sight picture, trigger control, and follow-through must be made reflexive actions through dry practice.

Only then can meaningful development result from actual firing drills.

ing sight alignment, sight picture, shooting stance, grip, trigger control, breath control, and follow-through. Of these seven, four are most important for the tactical shooter: sight alignment, sight picture, trigger control, and follow-through.

Sight alignment is the relation between the front sight, the rear sight, and the shooter's eye. It is established by placing your visual focus on the front sight and aligning it with the rear sight (irrespective of any target). The top of the front sight must be seen as level with the top of the rear sight. Additionally, you must see equal amounts of light on both sides of the front sight as viewed through the rear sight notch.

This describes perfect vertical and horizontal alignment of the sights and is what we always would like to have. Sometimes we will settle for less if the target is close enough. Generally, the closer the target, the bigger it appears and the less perfect your sight alignment must be. Conversely, the more distant target (or the smaller target at close range) requires greater precision in sight alignment. In practice, however, *always strive for perfect alignment.*

Sight picture is the existing sight alignment as it is seen superimposed on the target's center of mass (i.e., the central portion of the visible target). Now let me ask you something. How many things can the human eye focus on at any one time? The eye is similar to a camera and can only focus on one thing at a time. With regards to the sight picture, there are three things that you want to keep in alignment—the target, the front sight, and the rear sight. Now imagine looking at these three points through a camera. If you focus the lens on the front sight, you can still see the target well enough, although it appears somewhat out of focus in comparison to the front sight. Additionally, you can still see the rear sight well enough, although it too appears slightly out of focus in comparison to the front sight.

By focusing in on the front sight, you can see both the target and the rear sight well enough in your peripheral vision (although not as clear and focused as the front sight) to keep all three points in alignment. That is the "secret" of sight picture. The more difficult the shot is (i.e., distant or small target), then the more precise that sight picture must be. The visual and mental focus must always remain on the front sight.

Another important aspect of the sight picture is whether you should close the nondominant eye or keep both eyes open. The simple fact of the matter is that most students I've seen cannot focus on the front sight as well if both eyes are kept open. If it's not an issue for you, don't worry about it. If you find it difficult to focus on the front sight with both eyes, close one eye. But which one?

We all have one eye that is more "dominant" than the other. That is the eye you want to use for sighting. For most shooters, their dominant eye is on the same side as their dominant hand. In other words, a right-handed shooter's dominant eye will most likely be his right one, and vice versa. Some shooters are cross-eye dominant, i.e., right-handed and left eye dominant, and vice versa.

Here is how you find out which eye is dominant. Make a

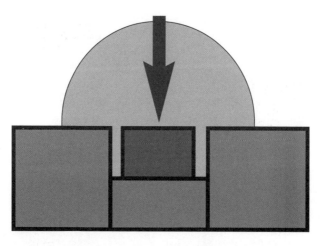

This is the perfect sight picture. It is formed by superimposing perfect sight alignment on the desired impact point. The tip of the vertical arrow designates the point upon which you must place your visual and mental focus.

small OK sign with your primary hand and look at a target through the opening with both eyes open. Now close the eye that is opposite to your primary hand. If the target did not disappear from view, your primary side eye is dominant. If it did disappear, your support side eye is dominant.

If your primary side eye is dominant, you simply close the support side eye when focusing on the front sight. If your dominant eye is on the support side, you have two options. Either close the eye that is opposite of your primary side and learn to sight with the nondominant eye, or close that nondominant eye and modify your shooting position slightly by angling the head slightly to allow the support side eye access to the sights.

Those of you who may have been schooled to keep both eyes open, take notice. The reason given for not closing one eye is that you may need it to see things around you, but this is hardly a combat reality. The nondominant eye is shut for only fractions of seconds while shots are fired, so in reality

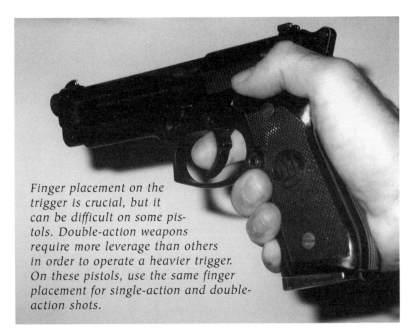

Finger placement on the trigger is crucial, but it can be difficult on some pistols. Double-action weapons require more leverage than others in order to operate a heavier trigger. On these pistols, use the same finger placement for single-action and double-action shots.

you are not missing anything of your immediate surroundings. If you are faced with a hostile man intent on killing you, to survive and win you must do him before he does you. In such instances, do you really think you will be looking around with your nondominant eye for other adversaries? Of course not! You will be too busy with the problem at hand to worry about other potential problems out there somewhere.

So this is the sequence of events. Your eyes are initially focused on the target, specifically on the center of mass. The pistol is raised up into the line of sight between the eye and the target. The nondominant eye is closed to allow the dominant eye to focus better on the front sight. Sight alignment is verified by bringing the visual focus to the front sight, as seen through the rear sight notch, and as the two points of reference are aligned on the target's center of mass. As the eye focuses clearly on the front sight, the rear sight and the target will be visible in the foreground and background but will be slightly out of focus. You must see the front sight with

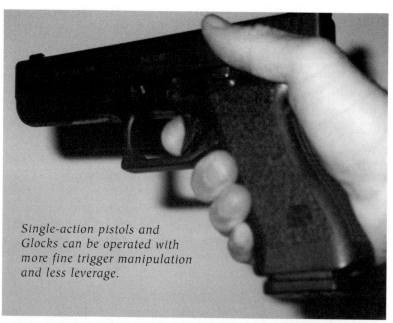

Single-action pistols and Glocks can be operated with more fine trigger manipulation and less leverage.

Unless your pistol has an overly heavy trigger (which is detrimental to surgical marksmanship), there is no need for a lot of finger leverage or for a convulsive hold such as this one.

crystal clarity and sharp enough focus to be able to count the serrations on it. Moreover, you must concentrate your mental focus on that front sight to exclusion of all else around you (more on this later, Grasshopper). This keeps the pistol on target.

The third fundamental, and probably the most important, is trigger control. Proper trigger control allows the shooter to fire a shot without disturbing the sight picture. The trigger must be pressed smoothly to the rear, without any disturbance of the sight picture, until the pistol discharges. Two key elements to this are finger placement and the surprise break.

Correct finger placement on the trigger is dependent on the type of trigger you are operating. Some triggers are naturally easier to operate than others, but all can be managed with enough training. With Colt/Browning single-action triggers, the area of the first pad of the finger seems to work best. When using a Glock pistol, the area between the pad and the first joint will allow you the best control. Finally, if you are using a double-action pistol, you must place much more finger on the trigger in order to provide the leverage necessary to operate the heavier trigger. For these guns the area just above the first joint will work best.

The finger placement should allow you to press straight to the rear without any lateral divergence in pressure. Placing too much of the finger or, conversely, not enough finger on the trigger will cause your shots to string laterally. Such extremes in placement will cause you to exert pressure to the side as well as the rear of the trigger, with poor results on target.

Before we discuss the actual operation of the trigger, I want to discuss physiology and firearm discharge. The fact is, it is unnatural to us to experience a small explosion out there at the end of our hand. That is precisely what happens when we shoot, right? Invariably then, our subconscious mind wants us to flinch, close our eyes, and do all manner of silly things in anticipation of the forthcoming big bang. This creates all sorts of problems with marksmanship. Not to worry, however, as we can easily get around this by allowing the shot to "surprise" us.

When operating a trigger, the shooter applies smooth and constant pressure until eventually and almost unintentionally, the pressure is sufficient to "break" the trigger. This is called a surprise break. Pressing the trigger in this manner may be likened to using an eyedropper. Think of the process involved. You "align" the dropper above your eye, you get the proper "sight picture" by focusing on the end of the eyedropper, and you gradually begin increasing pressure until one drop forms and falls into the eye, almost by surprise. If you force the drop out by mashing the eyedropper, you will flinch, close the eye, and get the drops everywhere except where you want them to go.

The same process applies to operating the trigger on a pistol. First, align the sights with the target and establish an appropriate sight picture. Next, focus visually on the front sight while building constant smooth pressure on the trigger until eventually the pistol fires by surprise.

Of paramount importance is that you do not specifically expect the break of the trigger. You know that it is going to occur, and you maintain constant pressure on the trigger, but you do not want to know the precise instant when it will break. The trigger must break almost unintentionally. If you either anticipate the break or force it to occur, you will invariably bear down reflexively on the weapon and flinch at the final moment. This will cause the shot to go errant.

Remember when I said that the human eye can focus on only one thing at a time? Well under stress, the human mind is much the same way. If you mentally focus your attention (as well as your visual attention) on the top edge of the front sight while you operate the trigger, where will your thoughts be when that trigger pressure is enough to cause the gun to fire? They will be on the front sight, not on the small explosion that just happened. That is how you experience a surprise break, but most people do not understand this.

In a combative situation, you will not have an open-ended time interval in which to press the trigger so very carefully. This does not, however, invalidate or change the process. Going back to the eyedropper analogy, those of you who put drops in your eyes on a daily basis know that it becomes quite easy as you get used to the procedure. As you become accomplished at using the eyedropper, you do not require the lengthy time interval to align, focus, and slowly p-r-e-s-s. On the contrary, it happens very quickly due to practice and familiarity. Operating the trigger on a pistol is the same. Through perfect practice and programming, you will operate the trigger in the same fashion and get a surprise break every time, but you will do it in less time. This is called the compressed surprise break.

The fourth fundamental, which is often ignored, is follow-through. Follow-through is controlling the pistol and the trigger after the shot is fired in order to avoid disturbing the alignment of the pistol. When actually firing a shot, you will visually lose the front sight momentarily on recoil. As soon as the recoil dissipates, regain front sight focus immediately. Additionally, do not release the trigger until the recoil cycle is complete. Maintain finger contact on the trigger and hold it to the rear as the shot is fired. Release it only after you have reacquired the front sight.

The ability to fire an additional controlled shot is extremely important in a tactical situation. Except for special circumstances such as single, precise head shots, you will usually fire twice. The reasons for this are to enhance the damage on the target as well as to ensure at least one hit under the stressful conditions of a life-threatening situation.

The way to fire that second shot quickly is to release the trigger only far enough to reset it via the disconnector device in each pistol. The trigger will be reset when you hear the audible (and feel the tactile) "click" as you release. At this point you should have already refocused on the front sight just as you did for the first shot and simply begin the pressure build-up with the trigger finger again until you experience a second surprise break. This is called a controlled pair. Each of the two shots is a controlled, individual shot. Each one requires a separate sight picture and a separate surprise break, even if executed very quickly.

These are the secrets of marksmanship. Study them well, as they are the keys to hitting. In the end, they are the keys to your survival.

CHAPTER 10

THE READY POSITION

Nobody in the world is fast enough to draw and shoot an attentive adversary who has the drop on you. When you have prior warning that a fight is on the evening's activity list, it is far better to have the pistol in hand than in the holster. If this will be the case, then it is also advisable to hold it in some form of ready position.

Understand that a ready position is a ready-to-shoot-position, not a resting position. A sound ready position allows you to bring the pistol up on target and solve the problem with a minimum of fuss and fanfare.

There are a number of suitable ready positions for specific circumstances. For the purposes of this text, we will use the standard ready position, also known as the low ready.

To acquire the low ready position, get into the same upper body attitude as your shooting stance. Now simply lower the muzzle, without relaxing the position of the arms, until the pistol is oriented 45 degrees below horizontal. This allows you to scan for adversaries and to assess potential threats without the weapon blocking your view of things.

At times when you are facing a specific threat, simply raise the pistol halfway up so that it is approximately halfway between the low ready and on target. The muzzle is oriented approximately at a point where you can see the hands of the bad guy.

The last thing you want to do is walk around with your muzzle pointing to the ground and the weapon extended outwards.

The Ready Position

For most situations, a ready position with the muzzle held at about 45 degrees will work well.

The instant you have an adversary in front of you, get the muzzle up and on him. Your finger is not on the trigger and the muzzle can easily be lowered again.

This "contact ready" position has been a source of controversy among many trainers, and I may as well address the issues now. The points used against the contact ready are:

1) "The pistol held high obscures the target, and you can't see him." This is simply not true if you acquire the position properly. The pistol is not pointed at the target but rather is held about one-half to three quarters of the way up from low ready, leaving you plenty of room to see what's going on. Not only does this make you about .50 seconds faster to target, but it also minimizes the "overswing" that often results when presenting from the low ready under stress.

2) "Using the contact ready endangers the adversary." Yes, but so what? If I face a man who has concerned me enough to draw my pistol, I sure as hell want him to feel "endangered" enough to stop his actions, wouldn't you? You can't have it both ways: you are either a threat to your adversary, or you are not. I want to be as threatening as possible to my enemy. There is no political correctness in a gunfight!

In close quarters, the ready position can be "shortened" in this way.

3)   "If you point a pistol at an adversary, he will be fixated on it and will not listen to your verbal instructions." Quite the contrary. I've found that subjects who do not need to be shot are much more compliant if you show them a clear intention to shoot if they do not comply. This is much more evident with a contact ready gun than a low ready gun. The low ready gun may, in fact, be viewed as a reluctance on the operator's part to use deadly force. Such a conveyed attitude may actually cause a confrontation to escalate.

4)   "To teach two different kinds of readies is unrealistic, and the contact ready is unlikely to be used because it is unnatural." Again, I disagree. We teach three different types of malfunction clearance methods, two or three types of reloads (depending on the school), and a number of close quarters emergency responses. Each tool exists for a specific problem. The contact ready is suitable for some problems and not for others, just as the low ready is suitable for some problems and not others. Training is what will make the difference. A man who trains with only one ready will revert to that in time of crisis, even if something else is called for.

To support this study, I thought back to the many times I've taken suspects at gunpoint in both shooting and non-shooting situations. Not one of them was taken at low ready; *all* were at contact ready. Moreover, I discussed this with colleagues who've yanked on the elephant's tail (police officers, private citizens, and soldiers) and, to a man, they used the contact ready. Perhaps dismissing the contact ready in favor of using the low ready exclusively is a sure sign of too much controlled environment training.

When a threat is realized, the presentation from the ready position begins with your eyes on target and your finger off the trigger. Once again, do not rely on keeping it off the trigger! Rather, find some tactile index point on the pistol's frame to place that finger on. That way there is no question about what "off" means—the finger is either on the trigger or it is on the index point. Additionally, if your pistol incorporates a safety lever, such as with a Colt/Browning pistol, you must place your thumb on that lever, ready to disengage it on the way up.

Now, raise the pistol up into the line of sight, align the sights, and superimpose them on the target. Take up the slack on the trigger and bring the visual focus sharply to the front sight. See the front sight in crystal clear focus as you begin the final pressure on the trigger. Eventually (it could take less than a second or it could take more, depending on the circumstances and difficulty of the shot), the pressure on the trigger will suffice to cause the pistol's firing mechanism to fire a shot. When this happens, you must automatically regain visual focus on the front sight and reset the trigger. Self-defense situations often require firing at least two shots, so stay ready.

When operating pistols equipped with double-action triggers, the trigger finger must take up the little bit of free travel at the start of the trigger movement. Note that this is not "stacking" the trigger, an old method for operating double-action revolvers whereby the shooter rolls back the trigger just short of the point of no return and then pauses to stabilize his sights. What I'm talking about here is simply taking up the travel evident in each trigger before the pressure begins to move the hammer at all. When the "final" press is made, a double-action shooter will have to press the trigger completely through the process whereby the hammer is cocked and released. This requires a smooth and not excessively heavy trigger.

After you've fired a couple of shots, a real adversary will not just stand there, ready for evaluation, like the paper targets do at the range. He will either have fallen after a good solid hit, he will have been unaffected by the shot, or he will have moved. In reality, you will probably be able to determine his status without moving your pistol. Just because you are focusing on the front sight does not mean that the adversary will simply disappear.

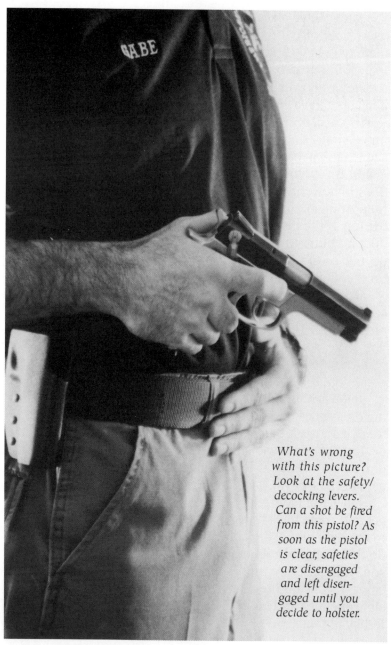

What's wrong with this picture? Look at the safety/decocking levers. Can a shot be fired from this pistol? As soon as the pistol is clear, safeties are disengaged and left disengaged until you decide to holster.

After you've placed the first two rounds into the target area, allow your visual focus to travel to the adversary. If he's still there, you have a failure to stop and must deal with it accordingly without debate. At close intervals (0 to 5 yards), you should be allowing the pistol to travel up to, and staging for, the head shot. (We will discuss this at length in Chapter 18.)

If you cannot determine the adversary's location after the initial shots, then you will need to lower the pistol so you can see what has happened and can act accordingly. If the pistol is still up in your line of sight, all you will see is the pistol. Start by lowering the pistol back into the contact ready position. At this point, your visual focus returns to the target over the top of the pistol. If he is still up, you'll automatically conduct a failure to stop solution from the contact ready. If you do not see the adversary, move the pistol to the low ready until you do see him.

Keep the visual focus on him for a brief instant to make sure he's out of the fight, but do not ignore everything else around you. Think the words, "Did I hit him? Did it work?" If you have not hit him solidly enough to put him down, you will know by now. Remember, regardless of the adversary's condition, if he's still a threat, shoot again!

If the fight is not over, don't be overly concerned about clicking on safeties and decocking hammers because some instructor demanded it the last time you trained. This is real life-and-death stuff, not some shooting school with range safety procedures that must be followed under threat of push-ups. The trigger finger, however, is off the trigger and on the index point.

Now, from low ready, check the area to the left of your target and come back to assess the adversary again. Then check to the right and again come back to the adversary. When you do this, make certain that your eyes and muzzle move in unison. The reason for this is to not only break your (now unnecessary) focus on the adversary but also to scan for other possible enemies and be in the proper position to deal with them if they're there.

CHAPTER 11

THE PRESENTATION FROM HOLSTER

Presenting, or drawing a pistol from a holster, is one of the most fundamental and important aspects of combat handgunning. A pistol, you will remember, is carried in case you get into an unexpected fight. If trouble is expected, you're better off arming yourself with a rifle, shotgun, or submachine gun. So bringing a pistol into action from a condition of unreadiness, and perhaps from under concealment, is its most likely deployment scenario and therefore paramount to this study.

Drawing a loaded pistol is an inherently dangerous activity. It should therefore be executed with minute attention to detail. The draw must first be learned in a step-by-step format in order to ingrain the proper procedures. When the individual steps and procedures are both mentally and physically memorized, you can attempt to smooth out the edges.

Under no circumstances should you initially strive for speed. Speed, you will find, is a by-product of smooth execution. Learn the correct procedure and practice it until it becomes as smooth as a reflexive act. Then, without even realizing it, you will also be fast.

Step one in the presentation is to acquire a firing grip on the pistol while it is still holstered. The firing grip is the same one you read about in Chapter 8. Be certain that you keep your finger *off* the trigger, holding it instead in a straight posi-

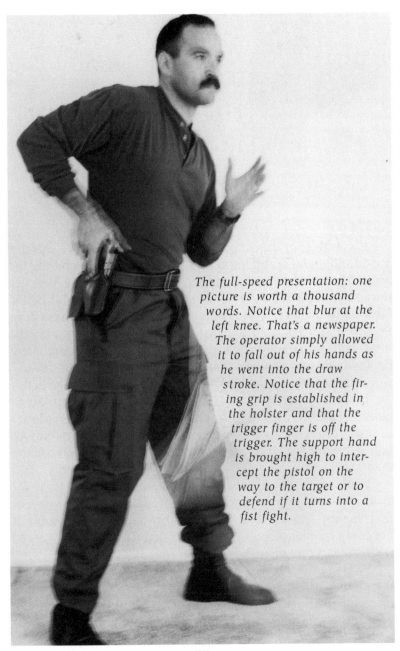

The full-speed presentation: one picture is worth a thousand words. Notice that blur at the left knee. That's a newspaper. The operator simply allowed it to fall out of his hands as he went into the draw stroke. Notice that the firing grip is established in the holster and that the trigger finger is off the trigger. The support hand is brought high to intercept the pistol on the way to the target or to defend if it turns into a fist fight.

The Presentation from Holster

The process: grip.

tion alongside the holster. If your holster does not cover the trigger guard, get rid of it and get a modern holster.

Simultaneous to the acquisition of a firing grip, the support hand takes a position roughly at the sternum. It is important to pre-position the support hand because it must eventually intercept the pistol on the way to the target. If your holster incorporates any type of restraining device, such as a strap or thumb break, it is disengaged at this step. Practice step one multiple times in order to program it into your subconscious mind.

Step two involves simply lifting the pistol clear of the holster. Be certain that you lift it high enough to clear the muzzle from the holster. The support hand remains in position. The trigger finger now moves into position at the index point on the frame but absolutely *not* on the trigger.

Step three requires pointing the muzzle toward the target and locking the pistol at the side of the ribcage in the close contact position. The firing wrist and thumb are actually in contact with the ribs just outside of the pectoral muscle, and the pistol is canted slightly outboard in order to avoid catching the slide on the garments if there is a requirement to fire. This points the pistol toward the target. The support hand remains in place, and the trigger finger is still off the trigger and resting on the index point. The primary hand is not advanced any farther. If the encounter took place at a close interval (within arm's reach), you would simply raise the support side elbow to intervene between the adversary and you, denying him access to the pistol as well as positioning for a close contact shot. For purposes of the present procedure, maintain the support hand in position at the sternum. (The close contact position, an invention of Southern California law enforcement, is intended not only as an emergency close quarters firing position but also as a final check before holstering. It is also useful for circumstances where physical contact is made with an adversary or when operating in close quarters environments during a search.)

Step four advances the pistol to the point of interception

The Presentation from Holster

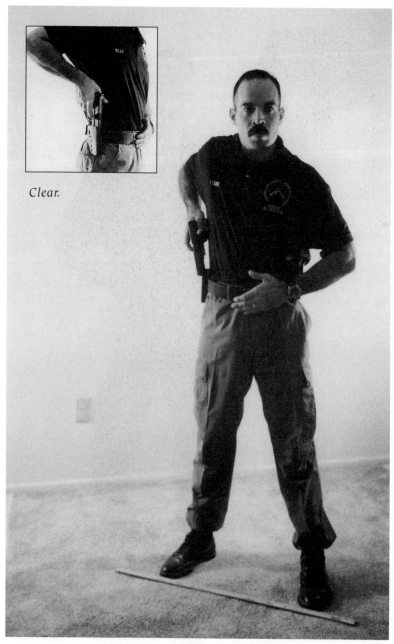

Clear.

Lock.

Up (sights, press, recover, etc.).

with the support hand. The hands move together into a proper grip and into the Weaver (or other) ready position. Safety levers, if any, are disengaged at this point. The firing arm straightens and the support arm bends at the elbow (which points downward). The trigger finger is still *off* the trigger.

Step five raises the pistol up into firing position. As the pistol begins to rise, the trigger finger finds the trigger and takes up the slack. The rest of the process—firing the shots—is pure marksmanship skills.

You may omit step four and present directly to the target if the situation requires it. In that case, the support hand intercepts the pistol as the primary hand comes forward and clears the body. Under no circumstances does the trigger finger enter the trigger guard or actually touch the trigger before step five.

After the problem appears to have been solved, proceed with the after-action assessment from the ready position.

"Did I hit him? Did it work?" Don't just give up after the shot goes off; make sure it worked. If not, shoot again. Don't holster until the threat is over or, in training environments, you tell yourself that it's over.

The Presentation from Holster

After you are certain that everything is secure, it is time to holster.

If drawing a loaded pistol is dangerous, so is holstering one! Holstering begins from the ready position. The trigger finger is always *off* the trigger. Those using Colt/Browning pistols will engage the safety but maintain the thumb positioned to disengage it quickly if necessary. Those using DA pistols with decocking capabilities now decock the gun.

Bring the support hand back to its intercept position at the sternum as you bring the pistol back to the close contact position. This does two things: it keeps the support hand out of the way during the holstering process, and it places the support side arm in a position from which it can launch a strike or deflecting motion if necessary.

From the close contact position, slowly find the holster with the muzzle of the pistol. Insert the pistol into the holster slowly. When the pistol is fully holstered and any retaining devices are refastened, the procedure is complete.

Do not be in a hurry to holster the pistol; take your time doing it. If you feel any obstruction in the holster during the procedure, stop and verify that it is clear. Forcing it may present you with a loud surprise if part of your shirt-tail has snagged on the trigger! As the Old West gunmen used to say, "Bring it out quickly, but put it back s-l-o-w-l-y."

Remember that all holstering procedures absolutely require that the trigger finger be held on the index point of the frame and off the trigger. Additionally, make certain that the muzzle does not sweep the support hand at any time.

Some readers may think that I am making too much out of this drawing and holstering business. All I can say is that the majority of negligent discharges occur during these two operations. If programming proper procedures does nothing else but prevent such mistakes, then it is well worth the effort. But this programming does much more than that. It ensures that you will respond in a like manner under stress. And that, my friends, is what this program is all about.

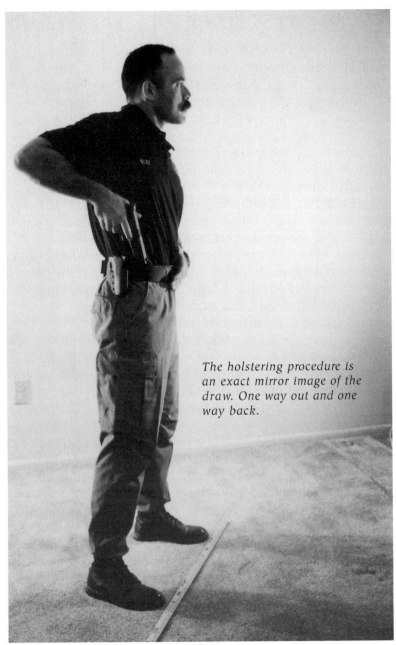

*The holstering procedure is
an exact mirror image of the
draw. One way out and one
way back.*

CHAPTER 12

THE TACTICAL RELOAD

The tactical reload is used to recharge the pistol to full capacity after a successful engagement but before leaving cover or changing positions. As noted, pistol fights are intense but brief. After the first clash, one of the parties will have either fallen from a hit or quickly disengaged. The reality is that you will probably never need more than the first few rounds in your magazine. In the interval after the initial clash, the fight may appear to be over as everyone on both sides waits for the smoke to clear in order to determine the next course of action. This lull in the storm is the best time to reload to full capacity. After all, it may not be over. You may be attacked again at any moment, so standing around with a partially depleted pistol is not a wise idea, is it? Certainly not! Therefore reload to full capacity and bring the pistol to the ready position so you can actually see what is going on.

Let's look at this situation closely. There is no immediate need to shoot, and there are no visible targets. But what will your mental state be? Remember that you have probably just shot another human being who only seconds before was doing his best to kill you! You are going to be agitated, shaky, and full of adrenaline. Any gun handling procedure *must* consider this reality.

There are other versions of the tactical reload (as well as other gun handling maneuvers) that were conceived in the controlled environment of the shooting range by persons whose intentions may have been honest enough but whose experience never included the very real issues of performing under life-or-death pressure. Still others were developed by men who simply wanted to put their name on something that was "different." These methods may appear faster and more efficient under controlled conditions, but add the factors present in a stress-filled environment where losing means dying and they will quickly fail.

The tactical reload described below is designed to work under the stress of a gun battle. In essence, it involves juggling three items: the pistol, the depleted magazine, and the replacement magazine. Now, let me ask you one of those pivotal questions: which of the three is most important? If you answered the pistol, then you are quite correct. Your pistol is your life—don't drop it! This means that if you can avoid altering the firing grip in any way, then avoid it. Secondary in importance is the replacement magazine, and last in importance is the depleted magazine.

The tactical reload should follow standard loading procedures as far as the grip on the magazine and the method of insertion are concerned. While it would be nice to keep the depleted magazine for later use, and while most techniques allow this, it is not the end of the world if you drop it.

I've learned just about everyone's version of the tactical reload (and boy there are a few). I haven't invented any or named any after myself, so I have no secret agenda other than to choose the best one. I believe that is the one described here.

From the ready position, the support hand leaves the pistol and obtains a fresh magazine from the belt. The support hand brings that magazine underneath the pistol and positions the palm about half a magazine length below the bottom of the pistol, prepared to catch the on-board magazine upon ejection. The support hand's index finger is positioned along the front of the magazine. Simultaneously, the pistol is slightly angled in the primary hand in order to allow the primary hand thumb to operate the magazine release button.

Begin at the ready position.

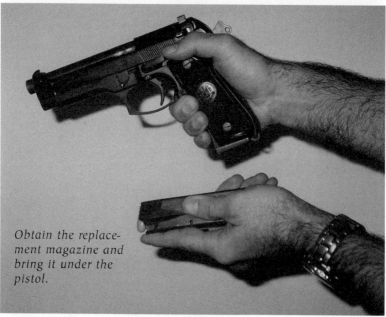

Obtain the replacement magazine and bring it under the pistol.

The depleted magazine is ejected into the support hand palm and the fingers curl toward the body, trapping it between the second and third fingers. The support hand then rotates slightly, aligning the replacement magazine with the magazine well, and inserts it into the pistol in the usual manner. This avoids confusing the magazines.

The replacement magazine is retained between the fingers of the support hand as it re-acquires the two-handed grip on the pistol. Both hands grip the pistol at the ready position and tactical operations are resumed if necessary. If not, then the depleted magazine is secured in a pocket or pouch.

If you carry a number of magazines, then putting the depleted magazine back into the pouch may not be advisable lest you confuse it for a fully loaded one later in the fight, with potentially disastrous results. If you carry only one spare, however, put it right back into the pouch, as loading with something is better than having nothing to load.

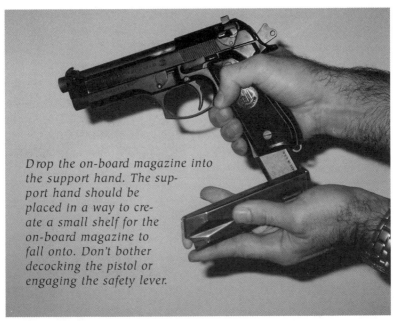

Drop the on-board magazine into the support hand. The support hand should be placed in a way to create a small shelf for the on-board magazine to fall onto. Don't bother decocking the pistol or engaging the safety lever.

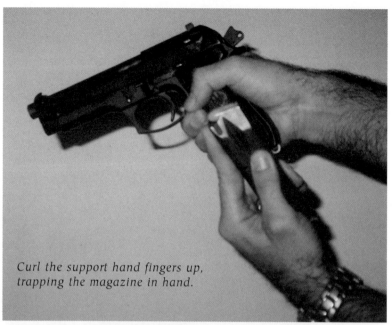

Curl the support hand fingers up, trapping the magazine in hand.

This is how it should look.

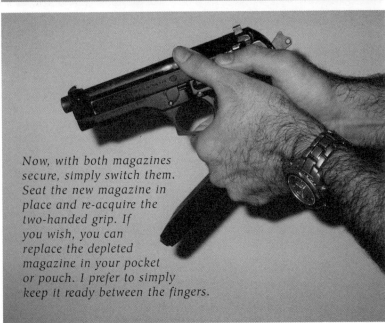

Now, with both magazines secure, simply switch them. Seat the new magazine in place and re-acquire the two-handed grip. If you wish, you can replace the depleted magazine in your pocket or pouch. I prefer to simply keep it ready between the fingers.

CHAPTER 13

THE SPEED RELOAD

Although the tactical reload will likely be used more than the speed reload, it is important to know how to recharge a completely empty pistol just in case. There are times when you may shoot every single round in your pistol because it was a tactical necessity. At such times, the first indication that your pistol is empty will be a slide that has locked back on an empty magazine. This is solved by the out-of-battery speed reload.

What you will see is simply your slide out of battery. Now this could mean several things, all of which initially appear to be the same problem, but each of which has its own solution. This means that you must identify the problem before deciding on its solution. For example, if you have a failure to eject (AKA, a stovepipe malfunction), reloading the pistol will not help.

The first step in this (and any other) reactive gun handling maneuver is to cant the muzzle slightly upward and *look* at the ejection port area to determine the problem. What will you see in the case of a dry weapon? Absolutely nothing. There will be an empty chamber and the follower of the empty magazine.

This will invariably happen as you are shooting an adversary who is also shooting at you, and there will be a very urgent need to get back into the fight. The sport competition method of dropping the empty magazine while retaining a round in the chamber is not tactically sound in this situation. Think about it. If you had one round in your pistol and there was one adversary standing in front of you, should you A) drop the magazine and execute a speed load, or B) shoot him with the last round and reload the empty and out of battery pistol? The answer, of course, is B!

Unlike with the tactical reload, when you recognize that your pistol is empty in a deadly situation there will be an urgent need to keep shooting that supercedes saving a partially depleted magazine. This means that the pistol remains *up* and *on target* so that you may resume shooting immediately if necessary.

Keeping the pistol on target, the support hand leaves the pistol and obtains a fresh magazine. Again, it is important to index the magazine with the index finger along the front to maintain continuity of technique wherever possible. Simultaneously, the primary hand angles the pistol slightly in order to access the magazine release button with the thumb as well as placing the mag well at the same angle as the forthcoming magazine. This angle is about 11 degrees.

When the support hand has the replacement magazine in hand from the pouch, the primary hand ejects the empty magazine. The timing is simultaneous. The support hand immediately brings the replacement magazine up toward the pistol and indexes the flat back of the magazine against the flat back of the magazine well. This occurs very quickly, and the replacement magazine on the way to the pistol actually passes the empty one as it drops to the ground. The next step is simply to roll the magazine into place and seat it with one firm push.

The final issue is that of releasing the slide. If you can release the slide by reaching up with the primary hand and disengaging the slide latch, you'll find that it is faster than the other methods. The only problem is that sometimes you will be so fast that you will release the slide before the magazine is fully seated. You will now have a weapon that is still

96

The Speed Reload

The first indication you have that you are empty will probably be an inoperative weapon.

This could be due to just about anything, from a malfunction to, well, an empty gun. The point is that you have to look at it or feel what took place before you can fix it. When you look, you will see an empty magazine and chamber.

Reach and obtain a fresh magazine as you prepare to eject the empty one. Note the angle at which the pistol is now positioned.

unloaded for all intents and purposes. Finally, trying to do this when your hands are nearly frozen, wet, gloved, or even bloody will be a frustrating experience. I've found that the most positive—meaning the most Murphy-proof—method is to simply use the support hand to release the slide by sweeping over the top as you regrip the pistol.

Notice that I did not mention anything about shooting automatically at the end of the procedure. Training yourself to shoot as a conditioned reflex at the end of any gun handling drill is not wise. The reason is that the circumstances that existed prior to the maneuver might not still be in place. This means that your initial justification for shooting may not be there anymore. Shooting must always be a conscious decision on your part, based on what you perceive as a legitimate threat at the time.

Another type of speed reload is the in-battery speed reload. This one falls into the special circumstance category,

As you move the fresh magazine toward the pistol, you may eject the empty magazine. The two will actually pass each other midstream.

Insert and seat the new magazine.

Reach over the top of the pistol and cycle the slide back into battery.

You are now ready to go!

but it should be known and understood. In fast-moving tactical situations, an operator may be required to move quickly from one place to another during a lull in the fight. He may also be faced with having to chase an adversary immediately after shots have been fired. He may not be able to stop in order to execute a tactical reload, and accomplishing the tactical reload on the run is a precarious matter.

In this circumstance, he may execute an out-of-battery speed reload with an in-battery pistol. The only difference is that this is a proactive rather than reactive technique. Conceptually it is more related to the tactical reload, although the mechanics of it mirror the out-of-battery speed reload. Note that this method is used when there is no hostile target evident, but the requirement to move quickly precludes the idea of saving the depleted magazine.

Another suggestion: for training purposes, buy some practice magazines that will never be carried for tactical carry. This way you can drop them on the deck all day long without hesitation or danger of damaging your carry gear.

CHAPTER 14

MALFUNCTION CLEARING PROCEDURES

Every man-made thing has the potential to break or malfunction. When it comes to tactical firearms, this tends to happen at the worst possible times! It is extremely important to know how to clear such situations when they arise.

First, let's define a few things. A malfunction or stoppage is a problem that arises due to poor ammunition, operator error, worn or dirty magazines, and/or an extremely dirty weapon. These problems can be fixed immediately, while under fire if necessary, and the weapon brought back into action very quickly.

Problems arising from a broken or jammed weapon cannot be cleared in the field because they often require part replacement and generally must be attended to by an armorer. The "fix" for such problems is to, in order of preference, present your back-up gun, present your fighting knife, or evacuate the area. Evacuation is low on the list because oftentimes it's not an option mid-fight. While things are still hot, if you run they will chase, and remember that we are talking close-range confrontations, not when you are 100 yards away across the parking lot. If you have time and distance that's one thing, but often you will not.

The malfunction clearing methods described here are not only amazingly fast methods of getting your pistol back into action, but they take into account the physical and mental state that an operator is likely to be in during a fight to the death. Therefore, they are superior to what was taught in the past.

The techniques are designed in a symptom-solution format. Each problem has its symptom. When this symptom is experienced, the operator's programmed reflexive responses take over and implement the solution. For purposes of dry practicing these methods, it is essential to obtain some inert dummy rounds to use in setting up these stoppages.

Once again, you will notice that there is no reflexive shooting at the conclusion of these clearance drills. Programming yourself to fire without a conscious thought is not a wise idea. Chances are good that you will be required to shoot immediately as soon as the weapon is back in action, but this must be a conscious decision on your part, not a conditioned reflex.

The first malfunction is a failure to fire. This is also called a Type One stoppage. It is characterized by an audible "click" instead of an expected gunshot. The famous writer, Capstick, reported that this was the "loudest sound in the world." This stoppage may be caused by a bad cartridge (actually a bad primer), a magazine that has not been seated properly (therefore not feeding a new round into the chamber), or, in worst cases, a broken firing pin.

The first step after getting the "loudest sound in the world" is to *look* at the chamber area. The in–battery pistol coupled with the audible click are your indicators of the problem. The next step is to *tap* the bottom of the magazine with the base of your support hand palm, making sure that it is seated properly. Next, grab the rear of the slide in the area of the grasping grooves. Do not place your hand over the ejection port because doing so will prevent the ejection of any defective rounds in the chamber. Now *rack* the slide to the rear as you simultaneously flip the pistol to the right by turning your hand in a palm-up fashion. This will both extract and eject any defective rounds in the chamber. This movement of the slide will also chamber a fresh round and get you back into action. It is important to follow the racking motion and let the support hand move all the way to the firing side shoulder. This will condition you to activate the slide briskly as well as not ride it forward on the way back into battery. As soon as this is accomplished, re-acquire the two-handed grip and you are ready to determine if more shooting is necessary.

Type One Malfunction: Failure to fire
Symptom: A click instead of a bang
Solution: LOOK–TAP–RACK–FLIP

The second type of malfunction is a Type Two, or failure to eject. This has also been called a "stovepipe" in reference to the appearance of a partially ejected case stuck vertically in the ejection port. Unfortunately, this malfunction does not always appear as a stovepipe. The cartridge case is oftentimes trapped horizontally in the ejection port and is not as easily diagnosed (a muffler pipe?).

The initial indication that there is something wrong with your pistol will probably be that the trigger is not working. This will be followed by the realization that your slide appears to be out of battery. If you are lucky, you will see brass sticking up out of the ejection port. Don't bet your life on seeing the partially ejected case, because again, it may just as easily be horizontal in the ejection port, necessitating that you break your firing wrist enough to allow you to see into the port.

This is a wise course of action for two reasons. First, taking a quick look to see what you have will be what you do reflexively anyway. Second, a Type Two, from a shooter's eye view, looks identical to an out-of-battery empty gun and to a feedway stoppage. Each of these situations requires its own solution, and attempting to force the wrong solution often results in even worse problems. But the Type One and Two

As with an empty weapon, your first indication of a problem will be a failure to operate. Take a quick look to see what the problem is. This is the first step for all clearance maneuvers.

For either a failure to fire or a failure to eject, use the following method. Tap the bottom of the magazine.

Malfunction Clearing Procedures

Flip the weapon over to the right (that's where the ejection port is) as you briskly cycle the slide.

Allow the slide to chamber the new round as your hand travels toward the shoulder and you will be back in the fight.

clearances are identical, thereby saving time and effort! So the first step is to *look*.

What you will see is a spent case partially ejected in the ejection port. That is the visual stimulus. The solution from here is identical to the Type One. Why? Because a Type One stoppage takes one second to clear. Any other clearance intended to solve a Type Two failure to eject also takes about one second. Simplicity wins out, so we use a single maneuver to solve two problems.

It is important to actuate the slide all the way to the rear. This is better than the seemingly easier "sweep over the slide" method because a live round may not have fed underneath the spent case. Racking the slide all the way to the rear and allowing it to go back into battery guarantees a chambered live round.

To practice this clearing drill, lock the slide to the rear and place an empty brass case horizontally or vertically in the ejection port. Next, slowly ease the slide forward, thereby trapping the spent case. Now insert a magazine loaded with inert dummy rounds and you are ready to go.

Type Two Malfunction: Failure to eject
Symptom: Inoperative trigger, slide out of battery
Solution: LOOK–TAP–RACK–FLIP

The third type of malfunction is the "mother of all malfunctions." The Type Three stoppage is also called a feedway stoppage. This is a situation where two rounds are apparently competing for the chamber at the same time. It is characterized by a failure to extract or eject the spent cartridge case in the chamber, with the next live round feeding (or trying to) into position behind it. The indication of trouble will be an inoperative trigger. Moreover, you will immediately see that your slide is out of battery.

This stoppage is often operator-induced by improperly clearing a Type One or a Type Two, primarily by allowing the hand to cover the ejection port during the operation, thereby trapping the cases or cartridges inside. A worn or damaged extractor may also cause a Type Three. With some older design pistols, it may even be a defective magazine (I've found that modern magazines do not seem to be as culpable).

In any case, the first step, as with the failure to eject clearance, is to *look*. When you break your firing wrist and look, you will see a chambered round and a second round feeding in behind it.

The next thing to do is to extract the magazine. This will not be easy to do due to the tension created by the partially fed top-most rounds. Therefore, after looking to verify the problem, you must *lock* the slide to the rear. This will take the pressure off the magazine, allowing you to *strip* it out of the pistol and either abandon it or secure it in the primary hand between the little finger and ring finger. There are good reasons for both procedures, and I will not tell you that one is better than the other.

Discarding the magazine ensures that, if in fact the malfunction was magazine related, not reusing that magazine will prevent subsequent malfunctions. On the other hand, consider that you are, in effect, ejecting the magazine before you have the replacement in hand. If you've lost your other magazines due to violent physical activity (as happened to me some years ago), if the malfunction happens at the end of the fight (when all your reloads have already been expended), or if you face a late night grab-your-gun-off-the-nightstand-and-fight scenario (and do not have any replacement magazines with which to reload), saving the original magazine may be a desirable option. Choose one and stay with it.

On some pistols, such as the HK P7 series, it is extremely difficult to lock the slide to the rear. Other pistols may not incorporate a slide-locking feature. In such cases you must physically rip the magazine out of the pistol. This will be difficult to do, and it is rough on both hands and equipment, but you have no alternative.

After locking the slide to the rear and dealing with the

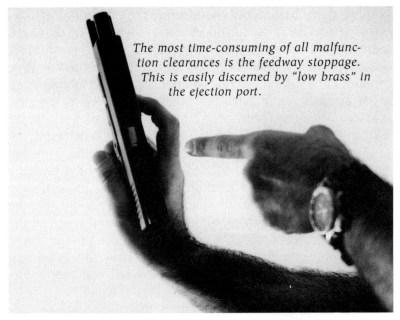

The most time-consuming of all malfunction clearances is the feedway stoppage. This is easily discerned by "low brass" in the ejection port.

Most pistols will require locking the slide to the rear to allow the magazine's extraction. Although some other methods may work with other pistols, be sure your chosen method works with your pistol.

The important thing is to be able to extract the on-board magazine. You may be able to accomplish this without locking the slide back, but it will be hard on magazines and fingers.

Once the magazine has been removed, clear the chamber area by cycling the slide as needed. Usually two or three times will do it.

Insert a fresh magazine.

Cycle the slide one more time to load and you are back in the fight!

Some pistols, notably the Glocks, can be cleared by pressing the magazine release button as you cycle the slide. This is very quick, but be certain that it will work with your particular pistol.

magazine (securing or discarding), you must clear all of the offending rounds out of the pistol by rack-rack-racking the slide three times. You now have a cleared but completely empty pistol. To get back into the fight, *insert* a fresh magazine (or the magazine in hand) and *rack* one final time to get back in the fight. A master shooter can accomplish this in 3.5 seconds. (An alternate method of clearing this problem is to press the magazine release button *as* you rack the slide three or four times. It saves approximately 1.5 seconds from the procedure, but it may not work with all weapon systems.)

To set up a Type Three for practice, lock the slide to the rear and insert an inert dummy round into the chamber. Next, insert a magazine filled with inert dummy rounds into the pistol. Ease the slide forward, partially feeding the topmost round behind the chambered round. It is imperative that you have a second, dummy-loaded magazine on your belt with which to reload during the training procedure.

Type Three Malfunction: Feedway stoppage
Symptom: Trigger is inoperative, slide is out of battery
Solution: LOOK–LOCK–STRIP–DISCARD OR SECURE–
RACK-RACK-RACK–INSERT–RACK

Eventually the issue of clearing malfunctions in extremely low light environments will come up. In the dark, you will not be able to see your pistol in order to visually determine the problem. The other side of the coin is that the adversary will not be able to see you either, so when your pistol won't go move out of there quickly! Once you are behind cover, feel the chamber area to attempt a diagnosis. If you cannot do this for whatever reason, execute the clearance for a feedway stoppage. This will guarantee to get the weapon back in action.

Although this may sound a bit esoteric, you will eventually be able to determine the status of the pistol by how it feels on recoil. A malfunctioned or empty weapon will feel different on the recoil than it normally does. This is no different to a driver recognizing an engine problem by how the car feels. This ability, of course, comes only after spending many hours on the range and will not come in a weekend. Try to be sensitive to what your pistol is doing during live-fire training sessions and you will learn to "read it" in time.

CHAPTER 15

360 DEGREE RESPONSE AND MULTIPLE HOSTILES

An adversary will often mount an attack from an unexpected area, such as from the side or rear, so you must have responses in place that allow you to orient your firing platform to any angle quickly and with a minimum of fanfare. It is important to move the firing platform rather than simply shooting the threat without moving the body. Not only might this bring you out of the line of fire, but it will also enhance your likelihood of getting hits before your adversary does.

The following techniques are described for a right-handed operator. Left handers should simply exchange the directions regarding right and left. Notice also that all of these techniques are useful from stationary conditions or while on the move as well as from the holster and from the ready.

Response to a threat from the left. Begin by looking at your adversary/target. (Let's be realistic, folks—you will always look first.) As you perceive the threat, step forward about a shoulder width with the primary side foot. Place your weight forward on the stepping foot. Simultaneously, obtain a firing grip on the holstered pistol. Now, pivot hard on the balls of the feet (particularly on the primary side foot) until you are oriented on the target. At the same time, present the pistol. Simple enough!

Whether responding to the right or left or behind you, the first step is always to move out of the centerline.

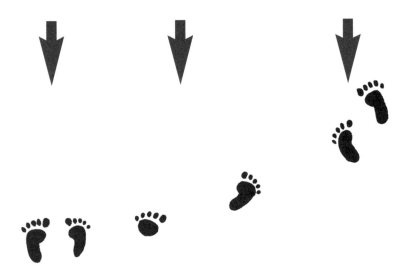

Response to an assault from the front. As the attack begins, move out of the line of attack as you move into firing position. Move along a diagonal line, not away from the attack. This can be to the left or the right as the situation demands.

Response to a threat from the right. Again, look at the target. Imagine that you are standing on a clock face with 12 o'clock directly ahead of you. Take your support side foot and step forward and across to the 2:00 position. Remember to place your weight forward onto the stepping foot, and pivot on it at the same time. Simultaneously, obtain a firing grip on the holstered pistol. Again, present your pistol as the pivot is completed.

Response to a threat from the rear. This time you cannot see your adversary because he is behind you. We will use the clock face analogy again with this technique. As the threat is perceived, step across with the primary side foot to the 11 o'clock position and place the weight forward onto the stepping foot. Simultaneously, obtain a firing grip on the holstered pistol. Begin to turn your head to look over your support side shoulder. This turning of the head will cause your upper body to begin to turn and your feet to pivot on the balls. As your body clears the turn and begins to slow down, the pistol is

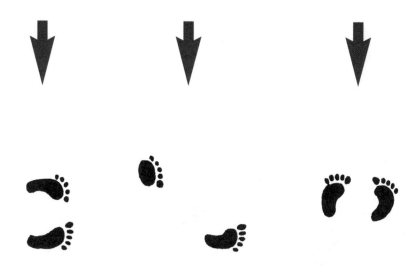

Response to an assault from the left. Get out of the way lest you be run over, and then respond.

presented toward the target. This is similar in execution as if you were walking away from a point and suddenly reversed direction mid-stride to walk back to that point.

A couple of warnings. First, for all of these techniques, do not draw the pistol before you turn. Doing so will create centrifugal motion with the pistol that will make it difficult to stop on target. This translates as a longer time interval to the first shot. Also, make the final movement a pivot, not a foot drag, and always step into known territory (i.e., forward rather than backward). These techniques must be useable on all surfaces from mud and snow to asphalt and linoleum, so watch your step!

Besides attacks from unexpected areas, statistics also tell us that we will often have to face more than one adversary. Therefore, it is important to practice traversing from one target to another. There are various tactical issues relating to multiple adversary situations, including lateral movement to

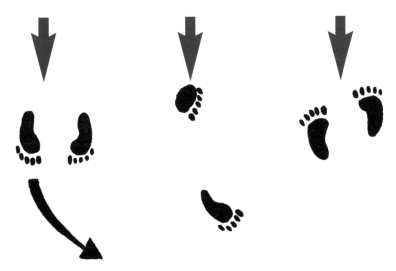

Response to an assault from the rear.

place the adversaries in line with one another, preventing them from firing at you simultaneously, initiating the confrontation rather than responding to their attack, and using cover to your advantage and their disadvantage. These issues are discussed at length in other volumes. For training purposes, we should practice the most difficult sort of engagement—when the targets/hostiles are standing side by side facing you.

Some trainers will advise shooting from one direction or another because that is the way we read or because that is the way the pistol recoils or whatever. Forget all of that. The real order of engagement will always be determined by the adversaries themselves. In short, the one who is most focused on you and who is most capable of killing you—in other words, the most immediate threat—will be dealt with first. This may require you to shoot right to left, left to right, or even inside targets to outside targets.

There is no secret to engaging multiple adversaries. As always, it's the basics and their application that will save the day. Find the first target and pick out the spot you wish to hit.

Bring the pistol to where your eyes are looking (from ready or from holster) and fire. If the targets are relatively close together, you will already have peripheral pick-up of the next target. The pistol and the eyes move together, stopping momentarily on target and pressing the shot. Continue with this until the targets are all neutralized.

It is important that as you begin to arrive on target, you slow down the pistol's arc of travel. If you do not, you will move too far and be required to bring it back on target. Think of when you are driving a car and you have your foot on the gas pedal. As you come to a stop sign, you normally take your foot off the pedal and allow the car to coast into position as you apply the brakes. It is the same feeling with the pistol. As you begin to arrive on target, let it coast into position as you get on the trigger and the front sight. As soon as the pistol stops, you are ready to fire.

Never try to sweep through the targets. The pistol must stop on each one before you fire or you risk missing the shot.

Never try to hit the first target with more than a single shot before moving to the next one. The basic rule of thumb is to hit each one as quickly as possible, then return to any who are still standing.

When the adversaries are very far apart, visually locate the next target first, then move the pistol to the spot on the target you wish to hit. In reality, we also do this when the targets are close together, but it is not as obvious as when they are separated by a greater distance.

A good drill is to set up two targets close enough together that you can see each one in the outer edge of your visual field without turning your head. Pick a spot on the first target and focus on it as hard as you can. Now quickly shift your visual focus and turn your head to the next target. You'll find that the visual shift precedes the head turning by a split second. Do this several times in each direction. When you are comfortable, add the unloaded pistol. This time, when you visually arrive on target, your pistol should already be aligned and the front sight should be clearly visible. When you are comfortable doing this with a dry pistol, actually shoot it. Remember, smooth is fast.

CHAPTER 16

USE OF THE PISTOL
IN REDUCED LIGHT

Students of small arms tactics who have studied the actual dynamics of armed encounters know that the vast majority of these incidents occur during hours of darkness. The degrees of darkness, however, vary considerably. Rarely, for example, will you be operating in a completely dark environment. Usually, some ambient light will be available, whether from stars or streetlights.

The real problem in low-light confrontations is target identification, not sight visibility as so many profess. If there is enough ambient light for you to see your adversary and perceive him as a threat, you may carry on with your response as you would in broad daylight. Eventually, however, the light levels will decrease to a point where you can still see your adversary, and you may even be able to perceive him as a threat, but you will not be able to discern your sights from the target as you seek the sight picture.

If the adversary is close enough, the simple alignment created by your firing stance will often be enough. (Remember, we are not talking about sniping but about rough shooting at arm's length on a very close and big target!) At this same light level, as the distance increases and the target gets smaller, you will require a more precise sight picture. This small window of light vs. dark is where the vaunted tritium night sights fit into place. These sights will allow you to locate your sight picture on a dark target against a dark background. You can't do that with simple black sights.

Beyond this point, the target will seem to blend into the background and your sights will too. Even tritium sights will not help differentiate between building and man, or hillside and man. For these situations, some tactical tips have worked for me and some of my associates.

If a man is firing at you from the darkness (and you are double damn sure that he is not a bewildered member of your own group, and you are certain of a safe background), you can use his muzzle flashes as a target indicator. You may not have a perfect sight picture or get a perfect hit under these conditions, but it is far better than wishing you were in Kansas with Toto again! You can also elevate your muzzle, use the lighter night sky for sight alignment, immediately align them on the adversary, and carry on.

This brings up another interesting issue. How many of you have tested your defensive/tactical ammunition for muzzle flash in low light? Just as you can use your adversary's muzzle flashes as a target indicator, he can use yours to locate and eliminate you! If your ammo produces significant muzzle flash, replace it.

When light levels get to this point, target identification is paramount. This requires a white light unit (that's tactical-speak for "flashlight").

The FBI was the first agency to address the issue of shooting in darkness. We tend to giggle and snicker at photos of those old-time G-men with their "electric torches" held out at arms length as they pointed in with their revolvers. Actually, this was state of the art with the equipment of the period. Those flashlights, you see, were a far cry from the ultrabright tactical flashlights of today. In those days they were called "torches" and were about as bright as a birthday cake for your grandfather.

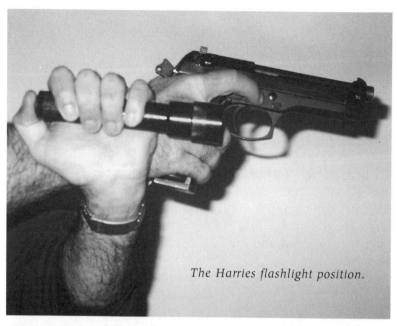

The Harries flashlight position.

The Harries position can be modified to any variety of "dual force" options as taught in our programs.

The idea of keeping this rather dim light at arm's length, for fear of its diffused beam highlighting your position, was not a bad one. The problem was keeping the light and the revolver pointed at the same place. So the arm's length method soon evolved into the side-by-side method. Again, this met with only a certain degree of success. It was a good modification up to the first shot; then the ever-present recoil of the shot quickly separated the two hands and the alignment was lost.

Things remained thus until the late 1960s, when a man named Mike Harries developed the flashlight technique named after him. Mike incorporated the dynamics of the Weaver stance into a method of holding the flashlight where the light is gripped in a "clubbing" grip with the lens at the bottom of the fist and the support hand wrist hooked around the firing hand wrist in a back-to-back configuration. This position not only allows similar recoil control to that of the standard Weaver stance, it also maintains a rough coaxiality between the pistol and the light before and during firing.

Other methods have been devised by instructors that are equally effective when practiced, including those by Ray Chapman and Pat Rogers. The Rogers method, promulgated by Surefire (the makers of the small super-bright tactical flashlights), is suitable for isosceles as well as Weaver shooters. It is best practiced with a Surefire Z-series flashlight.

The only development that far surpasses the efficiency and simplicity of the Harries or Rogers methods is actually mounting a light on the weapon. Commonly seen in the hands of special military and police teams, these set-ups work great and allow the operator to use his standard firing position. They do make the gun too big for concealment or general carry, but for a special purpose or home defense weapon, it cannot be beat.

The method to using a gun-mounted light in a tactical environment is to *avoid* using it as much as possible. Light is a target indicator. Walking around a darkened area looking for trouble with your light on makes you a lighthouse for

The Surefire/Rodgers flashlight position.

incoming rounds! Use the light sparingly. The best method is to light an area briefly, then move laterally in darkness. Repeat the process until the area to be cleared is truly clear.

If you encounter a threat and must shoot, keep your light on him for a brief instant after the shots arrive on target. This lets you know the results of your shooting in the event you have a failure to stop. If you fail to drop him and immediately extinguish the light, you won't know that you should have shot him again.

If you encounter a potential threat in low-light conditions and the rules of engagement do not call for shooting, what should you do? This is an issue of concern because most armed encounters do not end up in gunfire. Let's examine the possibilities. If you switch the light off or allow it to go off, your night vision will not have recovered in time to be able to see your adversary in the dark. Additionally, what do you think he might do? Who knows? What he will most certainly

A semi-permanent weapon-mounted tactical light is the best option for fighting in reduced-light environments.

The light will change the balance characteristics of the weapon somewhat, so be certain to practice with it.

not do is stand around waiting for you to reilluminate him. If you face such a situation, you must keep the light on your adversary, preferably aligned with his eyes, and control him with commands and so on from this position of advantage. Might your continual illumination of one man expose you to his compatriots who are waiting in the wings? Yes, that is certainly a possibility, but let's remember that a *present and immediate threat* must be handled with priority to other maybe-there-maybe-not threats.

The manual of gun handling with a flashlight does not differ from gun handling without a light. You must be able to perform malfunction clearances, tactical and speed loading, and any other circumstance that requires both hands. You therefore must secure that light somehow in order to have both hands free to manipulate the pistol.

One good idea is Surefire's lanyard arrangement for its lights. The lanyard was designed so that the user can secure it (and thus the flashlight) to his wrist, thereby freeing both hands for whatever needs might arise. The idea is to keep the lanyard tight around the wrist to minimize dangling. Also, if the lanyard is set too long you run the risk of tap-racking your brain housing group instead of your weapon during a clearance operation.

If you do not have or prefer to operate without a lanyard, the best solution is to simply place the light in your armpit (lens to the rear) and trap it in place with your arm. This gives you two hands to fix that which needs fixing. Having the lens point to the rear is imperative in the event that the light is inadvertently left on. By pointing it to the rear, any beam will be trapped in your armpit instead of becoming a runway light for low-flying incoming rounds.

I should mention what makes a good tactical flashlight. The best lights are the smallest but brightest you can find. The beam should be focused rather than diffused. An adjustable beam is fine, but a nonadjustable focused beam is better because it allows a bright spotlight, without gaps or dead spots, to be focused directly on the danger.

Along with size, weight is a factor. Lugging around a 5 pound flashlight may be a good idea for some people who are into caveman defensive tactics (unarmed jail guards for example), but most of us want easy-to-carry gear. So small, light, and bright are the key words!

Finally, a momentary on-off button is preferred to a standard click-on, click-off switch. If you lose control and drop a light equipped with the latter arrangement, it will invariably roll away and land pointing right at you, illuminating you for the enemy.

Is there a flashlight that has all of the attributes desirable for tactical operations? Yes, the Laser Products Surefire series of lights has what it takes. They are as small and light as a flashlight can be. They are brighter than any of the competition. They weigh about as much as a spare magazine for your personal pistol. They have a focused beam that is smooth and free of dark spots or rings. And they have the all-important momentary on-off switch that only turns the light on when the button is depressed. That's my choice.

CHAPTER 17

CLOSE QUARTERS COMBAT—SOME NEW IDEAS

Urban gunfights are short, intense events characterized by sudden violence at close range. The actual distances might astound many whose total close-quarters battle training program consists of "hammers" at 7 yards. You see, over 85 percent of these fights actually occur much closer . . . like within 10 feet! Many of them, in fact, take place well within arm's length.

Such close-proximity confrontations, rather than being "unthinkable," as one popular writer likes to call them, are quite the norm. Yet the dynamics involved in this type of fight are no different than those for any other type of close-quarters combat. As I tell my students, at such a close interval even a blind man with a rusty homemade zip gun can get lucky.

At these close distances, simply standing tall and drawing the pistol quickly is not sufficient. You must take into account how the dynamics of human reaction times affect your decision-action cycle. Generally speaking, the man who moves first, or initiates the action, will win, whereas the man who waits and reacts will usually lose. Simply put, marksmanship being equal, *action ALWAYS beats reaction*. If you stand and fast-draw when you see your threat, you will always be approximately a half to a full second behind the decision-

Rather than the typical 5 to 7 yard distance drilled at most training schools, this is how close the average gunfight may actually be.

action curve. At best, you'll shoot him an instant after he shoots or cuts you. Not a good situation, is it?

These action-reaction dynamics are unavoidable; it is simply how we are programmed neurologically. It was first described by the late Col. John Boyd as the Observation-Orientation-Decision-Action loop (OODA loop, for short). A fight of any kind is simply an event where each competitor observes his opponent, orients himself in relation to the opponent, decides on a course of action based on those observations, and finally acts out his decision. Whoever gets through that cycle the quickest has a remarkable advantage

> *To fully understand the dynamics and needs of the CQB environment, you must take a solid grounding in the fundamentals and place them under stress in a CQB training house. The student will quickly figure out that there needs to be a different set of skills for close-in fighting.*

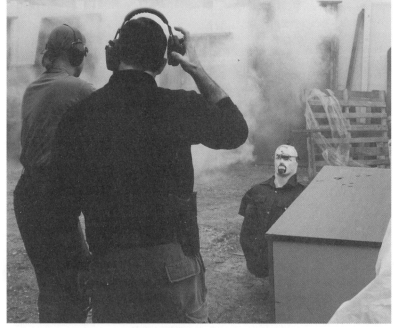

over the other fellow. An operator who is already at the action phase, for example, has a head start over someone who is still observing and orienting at the beginning of his own cycle. Things can be done to short-circuit or forestall the opponent's cycle, but we will get to those later.

Let's look at this from a practical perspective. Put yourself in this situation. You are facing your adversary at 3 yards (we'll be generous with the distance). He suddenly goes for the stolen revolver in his waistband as he yells, "Die, pig, die!" What do you do? Any potentially successful technique has to do two things at once:

1) It must allow you to get your weapon into action in order to cause sufficient damage and put the other man down, hopefully before he can carry out his mission.
2) It must also move you out of the line of fire, hopefully causing the other man to miss you with his initial burst of gunfire or getting you out of range of his knife or other hand-held weapon.

Just as your opponent went through his decision cycle prior to beginning his attack, he must repeat this cycle for every new and unexpected development in the confrontation before he can adapt to those changes. This may take just fractions of seconds, but that may be all you need. This is, after all, a business of fractions of seconds, where the slightest advantage may mean the difference between living and dying.

One answer is to condition a reflexive lateral side-step into your close quarters pistol presentation. This may be enough to move you out of the line of fire sufficiently to cause the opponent to miss with his first few shots or get you out of the way of his initial rush to close the gap between you, as the case may be. You've changed things on him, and he will be forced to reevaluate and alter his actions, but not before you get your own weapon into action. This simple side-step allows you to operate within his Observation-Orientation-Decision-Action loop. So would tossing your car keys in his face as you move and draw.

If the confrontation is closer, say within one step of physical contact, presenting the pistol to a standard firing position, even if preceded by a side-step, won't work. This will create a weapon retention problem for you and probably develop into an ugly wrestling match for your pistol.

Conventional wisdom says to simply step back and draw. I studied this method for years but have learned that there are other, better ways. You see, stepping to the rear only creates a gap where the adversary can simply step forward and gain ground on you. Additionally, nobody can move back faster than an aggressor can move forward. This is never a problem if you practice only on cardboard targets, which never advance on you. If you train with human adversaries using red training guns, you will quickly learn that an aggressive advancing opponent will simply run right over you, even after being hit. Even if the adversary were shot right in the heart, he'd still have enough momentum (not to mention oxygen) to crash into you.

To win, you must short-circuit the opponent's decision-action loop by changing his perception of the event quickly and drastically. Preceding the draw with a sharp finger jab to the eye, a palm strike to the nose, or even a simple palm heel to the chest will cause a slight hesitation, if not a complete rethinking of his attack plan. This may not, in truth, be a fight-stopper, but it will buy you time. The time you bought can now be used to step clear of him (to the rear or the side) and get your own weapon into action. If you've made your first step to the rear, be certain that any subsequent steps are made to the sides in order to get off the line of attack. This looks like an "L" shape if we were to draw it out on the deck.

In truth, pistol fighting at close quarters is conceptually very similar to close-quarters combat of any sort. To think that the presence of a firearm somehow excuses the user from the need to utilize *all* the weapons at his disposal—including his empty hands if necessary—is foolish and unrealistic. So training in a truly practical unarmed combat system is an excellent supplement to your pistol program.

Critics of the concept of blending hand-to-hand fighting skills with tactical pistol shooting suggest that operators must "either shoot or fight, but not both." They suggest that an adversary will simply grab your support hand (formerly called a "weak" hand) when you try to use an auxiliary striking/distraction technique. This indicates a naivete about the nature of actual physical confrontations. Nobody throws a punch and holds it out there for the cameras! These are quick, violent movements. At these distances, any strikes are unlikely to be blocked, caught, or avoided unless you are moving in slow motion. Even if the strike were to somehow miss the adversary, your hand will be back and away from his reach before he even realizes he's seen it. Remember the issues of reaction time when someone questions the need for a distraction strike.

Distraction techniques are still functional even if there is no maneuver room to the rear. In this case the distraction move is identical, but instead of moving to the rear, you move forward to the opponent's 10:00 or 2:00 o'clock area or even run right over him and then continue as usual. This seems contrary to the commonly held view to create distance, but you must realize that nobody can backpedal fast enough to get away from a close-range attack. You can't do it because you are not designed to run backwards!

What if he's closer? I mean really close. What if he's so close that he could head butt you as he discusses the fine points of your parent's doubtful relationship to the animal kingdom?

One popular technique that has been taught for years is the speed rock. This involves "rocking" the pistol out of the holster and rolling the torso back to orient the muzzle on target. For a long time I was a proponent of the speed rock. We got to the point where two quick shots could be placed into a target in three quarters of a second! This may be a useful technique if you are backed up against a table or vehicle, but I have learned that it is not a good idea even in those situations. Being a specialty technique, it should be reserved for special occasions, but even there it has some serious flaws.

Primarily, the classical speed rock's requirement to keep the support hand down by the belt instead of up in a fighting/defensive posture is extremely unrealistic. We've already discussed why moving back is not wise, yet the speed rock places you in an off-balanced position where flat-on-your-back is the only follow-up you have! Moreover, even if you successfully "speed rocked" a couple of rounds into your man, do you really think he'll just fall down in place? Hardly!

The speed rock has some glaring liabilities when looked at through the eye of a close quarters fighter (not just a close quarters shooter).

Even if he's been hit solidly, his own momentum will probably carry him right into you. In the rocked-back posture, you can't move laterally to avoid him, and you are not in a position of strength to absorb the collision. And forget about being able to respond to a failure to stop. Fortunately, there is an alternative.

The close-contact pistol position is suitable for extreme close quarters and has none of the failings of the speed rock. It places the pistol alongside the ribs, and the gun is indexed by having the primary/firing hand thumb and the weapon butt in contact with the torso. This, in turn, allows the pistol to be canted slightly outboard to avoid snagging on clothing or equipment. Additionally, it automatically orients the muzzle on the adversary's thoracic cavity area.

The torso is held erect in a strong fighting posture, braced for impact. The support hand is held in a fighting/defensive position, either out to the support side in a defensive warding-

A better alternative is the close contact position.

off manner or, preferably, elbow aggressively up and forward with the support hand protecting the pistol from above. This also places the fist in a position to execute strikes or other necessary functions while keeping it up and out of the way of the muzzle. These simple advantages of the close contact make the speed rock virtually obsolete.

The close-contact position can be acquired from the ready pistol or directly from the holster, and it can be directed to any point along a 360-degree circle. It is executed from a stationary position, but immediately after the first shots have been fired or contact is otherwise made, you must move. The first step may be to the rear, but any subsequent steps must be lateral to put some space between you and the bad guy and get you off his line of attack.

I conducted electronic timer drills and found that the close-contact position is just as fast as the speed rock. Tests with red training guns and human training partners showed that even if they managed to physically crash into me, I was in a position of strength, braced for collision, and able to maintain balance. It also allowed the ability to move laterally or even go to alternate body weapons. None of this is possible with the speed rock.

OK, so you've drilled the bad guy amidships two or more times from close quarters. Now what? The only thing for certain is that the fight has just begun. Don't call out for pizza yet! It's important to keep firing until the fight is over or until the adversary is no longer a threat. The idea that you should fire a couple of times and then stand around looking for results is not really a tactically wise procedure when you analyze it from a real-world perspective.

Again, the issue of reaction time is considered, both yours and his. Let's say you stopped shooting after a couple of shots and then, while you are readjusting your orientation to the situation, you realize you have a failure to stop. Furthermore, the presumed-dead adversary's pistol is now pointed right at you and he's about to fire. Regardless of what you do next,

When coupled with a simple but sound hand-to-hand repertoire, the close contact is a workable answer to any CQB problem.

Close Quarters Combat—Some New Ideas

Right: The close contact position is also viable for the various situations involved in a searching type mission, such as dealing with a closed door.

Below: At other moments, it may be desirable to simply lower the line of attack. This is common in martial arts circles, but combative shooters haven't yet figured it out.

you are now *behind* the action, and he is operating within your OODA loop. Even if you were able to fire right away, you could not stop him from shooting if he decided to fire.

In truth, at extreme close quarters you will know how your shots are affecting your adversary because you will probably be in physical contact with him. You shoot him; his attack falters; you are able to disengage from him. If your shots aren't effective, his attack won't falter and you may have to resort to combatives to break contact.

If you are able to buy some distance after the initial shots, your opponent will still be visible in your peripheral vision through your sights. You'll probably be able to see the effect of your gunfire, even if you are focusing visually on your front sight (as you should be at this point). It's important to keep firing while the adversary is still visible. This doesn't mean that you automatically empty your politically correct 10 round magazine into his chest but rather that after two to four shots, you should always stage your pistol for a head shot to ensure you don't experience a failure to stop . . . but that's the subject of the next chapter.

CHAPTER 18

FAILURE TO STOP—
THE SOLUTIONS

From somewhere in your throat, a voice you hardly recognize as your own echoes down the alley: *"Don't move!"* The pistol has already snapped into your hand automatically. Perhaps it was the hesitant look in your eyes or the way you avoided covering him with the muzzle of the pistol, but the three-strike loser, a veteran member of a violent street gang, was not convinced. You see his hands dart to his oversized waistband, five sizes too big. The prison tattoos on his muscular arms seem to move by themselves as his hands start to raise the stolen revolver. Quickly, you visually pick up a marginal flash sight picture on his chest and press off a quick pair. *POW! POW!*

Again, automatically you lower the pistol briskly to the low ready position, 45 degrees below horizontal, and prepare to assess the results. Fully expecting to see the criminal on the deck with two neat reddening holes in his chest, your elation melts into horror as you see the muzzle of his Smith & Wesson pointing at you!

Popular writers' comments to the contrary, all pistols are ballistically deficient. It matters not at all what you load them with: they are simply not very good at terminating human hostilities. This fact is widely known and recognized in the tactical community as well as by defensive minded citizens.

The utility of the pistol comes from its ease of carry, concealment, and handiness in close quarters. If you know that trouble is on the evening's entertainment list, with few exceptions you are better served with a rifle or shotgun. Sometimes, however, a pistol is all you will have when the show starts.

Anytime you deploy a pistol against a determined and aggressive human being, you *must* be prepared for the occurrence of a failure to stop with the standard response of two or three shots. While this chapter is not a treatise on terminal ballistics, suffice it to say that the statistical outcomes and known physiological effects of gunfire against humans are not in our favor, so we must expect the worst.

A typical untrained response to the "I Hit Him But He Didn't Go Down" syndrome is to simply panic fire the remainder of the magazine toward the adversary in the hopes that he will eventually fall. Such a course of action is rarely effective if the other man is bent on taking the fight to you. Consider how long it takes to fire 10 to 15 rounds into a target (and hit, of course). A man who has already absorbed a number of bullets but is still intent on firing his weapon at you or slicing your melon in two with his machete will easily do so before you can stop him with more body shots!

Why is this? After the human body experiences the initial trauma of the first few shots, it tends to disregard any further ballistic insult. In essence, the part of the nervous system that says "Fall down stupid, you've been shot" is no longer operational. Sure, the guy will probably die from the wounds, but he won't stop what he's doing right now. Even if the heart was completely destroyed, it could still take up to one full minute before, as my partners say, "all the oil drains out of the motor," and the adversary dies due to blood loss. Spraying more shots, then, is not the answer.

Another widely accepted solution if the first shots are not successful in terminating the discussion is a subsequent shot to the pelvic region to save the day. Popular belief has it that the adversary will fall down with a broken pelvis. While I agree that a man with a shattered pelvis will have a hard time building an assault, the hip bone is absolutely not connected to the trigger finger bone! A downed man may not be able to run up and tag you "it," but he can still press his trigger and kill you lickety split!

I am not a medical professional or a ballistician. My interests lie on the more pointy end of things. Wanting to know the "why not" of pelvic shots, however, I contacted an orthopedic surgeon (who is also a graduate of several shooting schools) for his expert opinion. He told me that the pelvis is a ring structure, and it would have to be fractured in two separate places for it to be unstable. Additionally, he said that the pelvis is a very substantial bone and wonders if a small-caliber centerfire rifle cartridge, let alone any handgun bullet, would be able to break it. He believes that in order to fracture this bone, it would have to be hit right on the points of the hips. Not much of a big deal until you stop to consider the actual size of the target area. The point of a hip is much smaller than the area on the human face where a shot should be placed for best effect. Hmmm. Strike two!

The third solution to the problem is the Mozambique drill. In our touchy-feely times, the alternate titles of "drug and body armor drill," or simply "failure to stop drill," are sometimes used. None of this can hide the fact that this technique was born in the small nation of Mozambique, Africa, during its turbulent years.

Jeff Cooper tells me that one of his students, John Rousseau, was on his way to the airport to catch the "last plane out" when he was set upon on the street by a guerrilla armed with an AK-47, complete with fixed bayonet! The insurgent charged at Rousseau, apparently intent on sticking him *en brochette*.

Rousseau, an accomplished pistolero in his own right, hauled out his Browning P35 and masterfully hammered the attacker twice amidships. Pleased with his marksmanship and quick reflexes, he brought his Browning down to admire his handiwork. We can well imagine his astonishment when he realized that his adversary was not nearly as impressed and was still charging!

Thinking quickly, Rousseau brought his pistol back into a firing position with the intent of shooting him in the brain. According to Cooper, Rousseau was a fine shot, but even the best of us would be somewhat rattled in similar circumstances. Rousseau was no exception. His last shot was fired in the nick of time, but instead of placing it in the command-control center, it was a little low—it entered between the clavicles and broke the spine. A severed spine is pretty conclusive, and the antagonist crashed to the dirt. Rousseau was quite relieved and wrote his friend Jeff Cooper about the incident. The Mozambique drill was born.

In the classic Mozambique drill, after two shots have been placed in the adversary's chest area, the operator lowers his pistol to the low ready position in order to view the results over the sights. If the adversary is down, the problem is solved and all is well. But if there is a failure to stop, evident by the adversary still standing or, in training environments, by the instructor's call for "head shot," the pistol is raised on target and a single surgical shot is fired into the brain-housing group.

But even this classic solution is not without its skeptics. It is one thing to pull this off with a certain degree of luck on the streets of an embattled Third World country or on demand against benign paper targets on the training range. To execute it against a similarly armed opponent who will kill you if he himself is not dropped is quite another.

The main problem with the standard Mozambique drill is a matter of reaction time. Nobody is fast enough to realize, first, that the danger is still present, then employ a solution in time to prevent the other guy from raising his pistol and firing at you after your shots had failed to stop him. The second point is that knowing the ballistic deficiencies of handguns and the likelihood of a failure to stop in conjunction with the dire consequences to you if you fail, shooting twice and stopping to evaluate the damage suddenly seems foolish! Even if you somehow destroyed the heart with your bullets, the adversary will still have from 30 to 45 seconds of oxygen/blood left in his brain to keep going. If he can get to you with his gun or knife, he can do *a lot* of damage within that window.

Think of it in terms of a street fight. Would you hit a determined opponent a couple of times in the ribs and then back off to see if it worked? I hardly think so. More likely, you will hit him until one of two things happen: either he falls down unconscious or you get too tired to hit him anymore! The same basic dynamics apply to gunfighting, accentuated only by the fact that you cannot afford to have him land any hits at all on you. The need to turn him off, to shoot him to the ground, is paramount. You can't do that with gratuitous body shots. You can, however, do so with a preplanned head shot.

After you place the first two shots in the thoracic cavity, automatically stage the pistol for the head shot. *If you see the sights superimposed on a face, you have a failure to stop.* At this point, the answer is not dependent on evaluating anything or trying to react faster. Seeing his face in your sights will only mean one thing—your body shots didn't work and he's looking right at you, carrying on with whatever threatening act that caused you to go to guns in the first place. Remember, we are talking about tenths of seconds here! All you know is that he attacked and you began shooting. Don't stop to evaluate the situation while he's still on his feet. If he's still standing, he's still a threat.

The question will invariably arise, "But what if he has dropped his weapon or is trying to surrender?" I'll tell you this—as soon as the fight starts, an atomic bomb could go off right next to you and you would not notice it because you will be too intent on hitting the other guy. Even if he were in the process of dropping his gun and surrendering as you were act-

This shooter has just fired a pair to the chest and his pistol's aim is travelling upward, staging for a head shot.

ing on his initial deadly assault, you would probably have already shot him before you could discern his subsequent intentions. To think that anyone would be able to have such trigger control and such visual perception as to see a change in posture or facial expression or a small black pistol dropping onto a black asphalt surface on a black night is too much. You will not have time to second-guess yourself after you decide to shoot. All the shoot/no-shoot stuff takes place *before* you decide to shoot, not during the act.

If you do indeed have a failure to stop, the adversary will not be standing there like a cardboard target waiting for your coup de grace. A real adversary will be in his "action phase," attacking or shooting. If you rely on the standard Mozambique/failure drill and stop in the middle of hostilities to evaluate the situation, you will be in the "decision phase." This is reactive instead of active and places you up to one full second behind the speed/power curve. You generally will not be able to react fast enough to make a difference if he presses the assault. On the other hand, if you've staged your pistol for the head shot, you are bypassing a large portion of the reactive phase without relinquishing the initiative.

Always remember: even though you must be ready to shoot an assailant to the ground, you are still conditioning yourself to *prepare* for the head shot, not necessarily to fire automatically. If there is no target visible when you stage for the shot, you will obviously not shoot. In this case, lower the pistol sharply to the ready pistol position; you most likely will find your adversary on the deck. Now ask yourself: "Did I hit him? Did it work?" If the answer to either question is "no," then hit him again until the answer is a firm "yes." Even if he's down, he may not be out. Again, if you see your front sight superimposed on his face as you stage for the head shot, you have a failure to stop and are in a solid position to solve it with minimal drama. If he's down and not a threat, look for his accomplices, as these guys usually do not work alone. Stay alert!

There are other solutions to the failure to stop problem that tend in the more aggressive direction. Some SpecOps teams requiring instant incapacitation of terrorists eschew any preliminary chest shots and advocate the cranial shot as Plan A. Don't dismiss the initial deliberate head shot for certain situations. It is a wise choice if you have prior knowledge of body armor or drug use or if you believe the adversary is in a heightened emotional state. The standard response of two to the body may be ineffective against such people.

A case to remember is the infamous Miami shootout between two dedicated bank robbers and the FBI agents intent on arresting them. One of the criminals absorbed enough lead to sink a ship but refused to fall down. He was able to murder two law enforcement offices and wound five others before finally succumbing to his own gunshot wounds.

Some instructors decry the head shot as a magnet for lawsuits. What a loss of perspective! Yes, you may have more explaining to do, but living to explain is better than lying on the ground as a bloody, gurgling mess and being liability-free. Lawsuits are bad, certainly, but so are funerals, especially if you are the star of the show. Primary and above all else, your goal is to win the fight!

There is another option that splits the difference between the reactive Mozambique drill and the premeditated head shot. I didn't invent it, although I often practice my failure to stop drill this way. I learned it from a Marine CQB instructor with extensive credentials in special operations. I have dubbed it the 2+1 drill, which describes how it is applied.

The Marine instructor said that the chest was the easiest and quickest part of the body to hit but, fully expecting a failure to stop, he didn't want to wait for any evaluation or assessment of results before proceeding to the head shot. He advocated placing two on board in the chest and immediately, without any hesitation or debate, placing a third shot in the eye cavity of the head.

This method has several advantages in terms of reactive/active speeds, effectiveness, and economy of force. By immediately taking the head shot without stopping to assess the body shots, the deficiency of the pistol is taken into consideration, as is the reality of action being faster than reaction. It solves the problem without any of the inherent drawbacks of the other proposed solutions.

The fear that the 2+1 drill will bring litigious attention is not as much an issue as some would have us believe. The head shot is widely accepted in law enforcement and military shooting disciplines as the standard response to the failure of previous shots or to resolve special situations. Explanations for your tactics may have to be provided later by you or your attorney, but they are certainly justified.

CHAPTER 19

THE PERFECT
PRACTICE ROUTINE

We've talked a great deal about what to do, so now let's get down to developing some reflexive skills that may save your life. Remember, your goal is to be able to perform each technique to physical perfection, not to adequate mediocrity.

For the following practice routine, you will need your pistol, two magazines, a holster, a suitable belt, and a spare magazine pouch. You will also need approximately 10 inert dummy rounds for your pistol. Once you have your gear in place, go through the dry practice safety checklist discussed in Chapter 6. Then set up your dry practice target on a suitable surface and stand back from it approximately 3 to 5 meters. If you prefer not to use the target included as Appendix B, an index card will do just fine as a dry practice target.

A word of caution regarding the operation of double-action pistols. If you are using such a pistol, you must be competent with both of its firing mechanisms, i.e., trigger cocking (or double action) and slide cocking (or single action).

In dry practice, pressing the trigger the first time will be done in the trigger-cocking mode. This does not address the following "shot" from a slide-cocked pistol because the slide does not reciprocate as it would in a live-fire drill.

In a gunfight, the first shot will be fired using trigger cock-

Strive for perfection in all your drills, and although you'll never be perfect, you'll come very close.

ing, but subsequent shots will be fired from an already cocked pistol. Most of the shots fired in such an environment are, in fact, fired from a slide-cocked pistol, or on single action. This must be addressed in training. Moreover, ignoring the slide-cocked trigger press will prevent proper follow-through in firing drills.

The solution is simple. Thumb cock the hammer after the first dry press and press again with a cocked hammer to simulate the difference between the two firing mechanisms. Another option is to have a training partner cycle your slide after the first double-action dry press. This will not only simulate recoil forces but allow you to maintain a firing grip as you follow through and reset the trigger.

EXERCISE 1

Face the target with the pistol at the ready position. Visual focus and attention must be on the target, specifically at the point designated as center of mass.

1) On command, briskly bring the pistol up to intersect the line of sight to the target. Mentally think the word "pause."

2) Align the sights by looking at the front sight through the rear sight notch. Close the nondominant eye and focus sharply on the top edge of the front sight. Simultaneously prep the trigger by taking up all of the free travel slack. Mentally think the word "verify."

3) While maintaining visual focus and attention on the top edge of the front sight, begin slow and steady pressure on the trigger until the hammer falls (or striker releases) without disturbing the existing alignment. Monitor your front sight for any lateral movement upon trigger break. Mentally think the word "press."

4) Maintain focus on the front sight for an instant after the trigger break. Mentally think the word "recover."

5) Now immediately bring the pistol to the ready position and extend your visual focus back to the target. The trigger finger comes *off* the trigger and goes on the index point. Watch your target as if it were a real adversary. Mentally ask yourself, "Did I hit him? Did it work?" Now, to break the target focus, begin scanning for other targets. Think "check left, check right."

Repeat Exercise 1 at least 10 times.

EXERCISE 2

This exercise is identical to Exercise 1 except that it begins with the pistol holstered and the eyes (and attention) on the target's center of mass. This drill executes the presentation in its five-count procedure.

1) On command, briskly obtain a firing grip on the holstered

pistol and move the support hand in place to intercept the forthcoming pistol. Eyes remain on target. Trigger finger is not on the trigger nor in the trigger guard—it is held in a straight position alongside the holster. The verbal command is "grip."

2) Lift the pistol clear of the holster by lifting the elbow. Nothing else moves or changes. Trigger finger is on the index point.

3) Roll the firing side shoulder back, thereby locking the pistol in a close-contact position. Nothing else changes. Trigger finger is on the index point.

4) The hands meet in the ready position. Trigger finger remains on the index point. Safeties are off.

5) Bring the pistol up to intersect the line of sight to the target. Mentally think the word "pause."

6) Align the sights by looking at the front sight through the rear sight notch. Close the nondominant eye and focus sharply on the top edge of the front sight. Simultaneously prep the trigger by taking up all of the free travel slack. Mentally think the word "verify."

7) While maintaining visual focus and attention on the top edge of the front sight, begin slow and steady pressure on the trigger until the hammer falls (or striker releases) without disturbing the existing alignment. Mentally think the word "press."

8) Maintain focus on the front sight momentarily after the break and monitor it for any lateral movement on the break. Mentally think the word "recover."

9) Now immediately bring the pistol to the ready position and extend the visual focus back to the target. Trigger finger goes back on the index point and *off* the trigger. Watch the target as if it were a real adversary and you were expecting him to get back up and resume the attack. Mentally ask yourself, "Did I hit him? Did it work?" Now, to break the target focus, begin scanning for other targets, thinking, "check left, check right."

10) Bring the pistol to the close-contact position as a final fail-safe check before reholstering. When you decide to move to the close-contact position, you may decock your double-action or engage your safety levers. Pause momentarily in that position. Slowly find the holster opening with your muzzle (*don't* look for it) and carefully insert the pistol into the holster.
Repeat Exercise 2 at least 10 times.

EXERCISE 3

Exercise 3 builds on the previous two exercises. It also begins with the pistol in the holster. This time, however, we smooth the rough edges and present from holster directly to the target. Before you attempt this one, be sure you've ingrained proper safety and handling procedures by mastering Exercise 2.

1) Eyes and attention are on the target's center of mass. On command, briskly obtain a firing grip on the holstered pistol and present it up to intersect the line of sight to the target. Make certain that both hands move in unison. Mentally think the word "pause."
2) Align the sights by looking at the front sight through the rear sight notch. Close the nondominant eye and focus sharply on the top edge of the front sight. Simultaneously prep the trigger by taking up all of the free travel slack. Mentally think the word "verify."
3) While maintaining visual focus and attention on the top edge of the front sight, begin slow and steady pressure on the trigger until the hammer falls (striker releases) without disturbing the existing alignment. Mentally think the word "press."
4) Maintain focus on the front sight momentarily after the break and monitor it for any lateral motion on the break. Mentally think the word "recover."

5) Now immediately bring the pistol to the ready position and extend the visual focus back to the target. Trigger finger goes back on the index point and *off* the trigger. Watch the target as if it were a real adversary and you were expecting him to get back up and resume the attack. Mentally ask yourself, "Did I hit him? Did it work?" Now, to break the target focus, begin scanning for other targets, thinking, "check left, check right."

6) Bring the pistol to the close-contact position and evaluate the area again before holstering. When you decide to move to the close-contact position, you may decock your DA or engage the safety levers. Slowly find the holster opening with the muzzle of your pistol without looking and carefully insert the pistol in the holster.

Repeat this exercise 25 times.

EXERCISE 4

Again building on the prior drills, Exercise 4 places the dry practice target to the left. You need not move the target; instead, simply take a half turn to your right. You will be presenting the pistol directly to the target from the holster. Left-handed shooters simply exchange the procedures in Exercises 4 and 5.

1) Begin with the dry practice target located 90 degrees to your left. Your visual focus and attention are on the target's center of mass. On command, step forward with your primary side foot and obtain a firing grip on the holstered pistol.

2) Maintaining your visual focus and attention, pivot on the balls of your feet so that at the completion of the pivot, you are lined up on target. As you commence the pivot, commence the presentation. Ideally, the pistol arrives on target as your pivot is completed.

3) Follow steps 5 through 8 from the previous exercises— PAUSE, VERIFY, PRESS, RECOVER.

4) Bring the pistol to the ready position and extend visual focus back to the target, expecting him to resume the attack. Mentally ask yourself, "Did I hit him? Did it work?" Look around for accomplices—"Check left, check right."
5) Decock DA pistols or engage safety levers on Colt/Browning/HK pistols. Move to the close-contact position. Find the holster with the muzzle and carefully holster the pistol.
   Repeat Exercise 4 at least 10 times.

EXERCISE 5

This is the flip side of the previous drill, this time with the target to the right.

1) Begin with the dry practice target located 90 degrees to your right. Your visual focus and attention are on the target's center of mass. On command, step across and slightly in front of your primary side foot with your support side foot and obtain a firing grip on the holstered pistol.
2) Maintaining your visual focus and attention on the target, pivot on the balls of your feet so that at the completion of your turn, you are aligned on the target. As you commence your pivot, commence the presentation. Ideally, the pistol arrives on target as your pivot is completed.
3) Follow the third step from the previous exercise—PAUSE, VERIFY, PRESS, RECOVER.
4) Bring the pistol down to the ready position and extend your visual focus back to the target, expecting him to resume the attack. Mentally ask yourself, "Did I hit him? Did it work?" Look around to break the target focus, thinking "Check left, check right."
5) Decock DA pistols or reengage safety levers. Move to the close-contact position. Find the holster with your muzzle and carefully holster the pistol.
   Repeat this exercise 10 times.

EXERCISE 6

This drill builds on the two previous drills and places the dry practice target to the rear. You will be presenting the pistol directly from holster to target after a 180 degree pivot that aligns you on target. This time you will not be looking at the target because it is located behind you, but you will strive to get your head turned and looking as soon as you can.

1) Begin with the target located directly behind you. On command, step across and slightly in front of your support side foot with your primary side foot. Simultaneously, turn your head to look over your shoulder and obtain a firing grip on your pistol.
2) Pivot on the balls of your feet so that at the completion of your pivot you are lined up on target. As soon as you pick up a visual verification of the target, begin to present your pistol. The pivot and the presentation should be timed so that they are both completed simultaneously.
3) PAUSE, VERIFY, PRESS, RECOVER.
4) Bring the pistol to the ready position and extend the visual focus back to the target. "Did I hit him? Did it work?" "Check left, check right."
5) Decock DA pistols or engage safety levers. Move to the close-contact position. Find the holster with the muzzle and carefully holster the pistol.
   Repeat exercise 10 times.

EXERCISE 7

The next exercise is the out-of-battery speed reload, also called the emergency reload. You will need a magazine loaded with inert dummy rounds in the magazine pouch on your belt. Insert an empty magazine in your pistol and lock the slide to the rear. You will be dropping the on-board magazine, so you might wish to lay a towel on the deck for it to land on. *Be sure to adhere to all safety procedures outlined in Chapter 6.*

1) Point in on the target with an out-of-battery pistol. Focus your vision and attention on the top edge of the front sight, as if you were conducting the previous drills. Press the trigger and notice how it feels. You see the slide is out-of-battery and "realize" that something is amiss with your pistol.
2) Break the firing side wrist and look into the ejection port. You see nothing. Think, "empty gun."
3) Immediately reach with your support hand for the magazine pouch on the belt and access a spare magazine. Simultaneously, flip the pistol in your hand far enough to be able to access the magazine release button with your thumb.
4) Press the magazine release button and eject the empty onboard magazine. Simultaneously, bring the replacement magazine up to the pistol. Ideally, both magazines will pass each other. As the replacement magazine reaches the pistol, index it by placing the flat of the magazine against the flat of the magazine well.
5) Roll the magazine until it is in line with the magazine well. Now seat it firmly in place. As the two hands come together into the firing grip, release the slide and chamber a round. At this point, your pistol is recharged (with inert dummy rounds) and on target.
6) Re-acquire the front sight as if you intended to press the trigger, but do not press it. Assess the situation instead. Bring the pistol to the ready position.

   Repeat exercise 10 times with the slide out of battery and 10 times with the slide in battery.

EXERCISE 8

This drill deals with the tactical reload. You will need two magazines loaded with inert dummy rounds. The reload will take place in the ready position only.

You realize that your weapon's ammunition is depleted and must be recharged to full capacity, but you have no targets to shoot. Keep your eyes downrange.

1) Move your support hand to the magazine pouch on the belt and reach for a replacement magazine. Bring that magazine alongside the pistol and prepare to receive the depleted magazine onto the palm between the middle and ring fingers.
2) Eject the depleted magazine into the support hand approximately two-thirds of the way out, catching it between the middle finger and ring fingers. It is important to not allow the magazine to fall all the way out uncontrolled. Roll the fingers toward the chest, further trapping the magazine in the hand, and extract it fully.
3) Roll the support hand a few degrees to orient the replacement magazine with the magazine well. Index the replacement magazine with the index finger straight along the front of the magazine. Placing the flat of the magazine against the flat of the magazine well, insert it fully and seat it firmly in place.
4) Secure the depleted magazine in the support hand and reacquire the two-handed grip. If you must reengage at this point, you can do so with the magazine still wedged between your fingers. After you have reestablished control of the scene, secure the depleted magazine in the pocket for later use.
5) Re-acquire the two-handed hold and ready position and assess the area.

Practice this exercise 10 times.

EXERCISE 9

This exercise addresses clearing malfunctions. As such it

has three parts, each dealing with one of the three major malfunction types. You will need two magazines loaded with inert dummy rounds as well as a handful of spent brass cases.

Type One Malfunction Clearance—Failure To Fire
Insert a magazine loaded with inert dummy rounds in the pistol, but keep the chamber empty. Begin with the pistol up on target, with your attention on the top edge of the front sight.

1) Press the trigger. Experience the "click" of an empty chamber or a defective round. That is the stimulus to execute the clearance drill.
2) Briskly tap the bottom of the magazine with the heel of your support hand palm. Immediately grasp the slide on the grasping grooves. Keep the hand away from the ejection port, and grab that slide strongly.
3) Rack the slide to the rear and simultaneously flip the pistol to the right.
4) Continue the circular motion with your support hand and reacquire the two-handed hold on target as if you intended to shoot, but do not press the trigger.

Type Two Malfunction Clearance—Failure To Eject
Lock the slide to the rear and turn the pistol ejection port up. Rest a spent brass case inside the ejection port at a right angle to the barrel. Now allow the slide to move forward, trapping the case. Insert a magazine filled with inert dummy rounds in the pistol.

1) Press the trigger and experience the inoperative trigger action. Visually notice that the slide is out of battery. Look to verify the problem. You see a spent case, partially ejected, in the ejection port.
2) Briskly tap the bottom of the magazine and position your hand at the rear of the slide on the grasping grooves. Make certain that your hand is nowhere near the ejection port.

3) Rack the slide to the rear as you flip the pistol to the right, clearing the offending case out of the pistol.
4) Continue the circular motion with your support hand and re-acquire the two-handed hold. Refocus on the front sight as if you were going to press the trigger, but do not press it. Move down to the ready position and assess the area.

Type Three Malfunction Clearance—Feedway Stoppage

Lock the slide to the rear and manually insert a single inert dummy round into the chamber. Insert a magazine loaded with inert dummy rounds into the pistol and ease the slide forward. This will cause the topmost round to feed in behind the originally chambered round.

1) With pistol up on target and your attention on the front sight, carefully press the trigger. Something is wrong. You notice that the slide is out of battery. Immediately break the firing wrist and look into the ejection port. You see two rounds competing for the chamber. That is your stimulus to proceed with the exercise.
2) Lock the slide to the rear.
3) Strip the on-board magazine out of the pistol and secure it between the little finger and ring finger of the primary hand or let it drop to the ground.
4) Rack, rack, rack the slide three times to clear out all offending cartridges and cases. You now have a clear but empty gun.
5) Insert a replacement magazine into the pistol.
6) Rack the slide one final time and immediately re-acquire the sights as if you were going to fire, but do not press the trigger. Assess the area.

Practice each clearing drill 5 times.

EXERCISE 10

This exercise deals with developing surgical accuracy for

close targets at close range. You will be presenting the pistol from the holster directly to the target. Specifically, your eyes will be looking at the center of mass of the target's head area.

1) Your eyes are on target looking specifically at the center of mass of the head area. On command, present the pistol directly to the target. Think the word, "pause."
2) As the pistol intersects the line of sight to the target, bring your visual focus and attention to the top edge of the front sight. Simultaneously prep the trigger by taking up the slack. Think the word, "verify."
3) Maintain visual focus and attention on the front sight and begin steady pressure on the trigger. Think the word, "press."
4) When the trigger breaks, keep focused on the front sight and monitor it for any movement. Think the word, "recover."
5) Drop the pistol to the ready position and think, "Did I hit him? Did it work?" Knowing that he is no longer a threat, check left and right.
6) Move to the close-contact position and conclude with holstering the pistol.
   Repeat exercise 15 times.

This concludes the dry practice session.

CHAPTER 20

DEVELOPING SPEED AND ACCURACY

Speed is very important in the tactical employment of pistols. Most often you will be responding to a threat, so you are already behind the power curve. Any increase in your speed is important. But I must point out that you want *controlled* speed. An Old West gunfighter once said, "No one was ever killed by a loud noise." That statement is worthy of note! Always remember that the purpose of shooting is to hit. That is paramount and more important than speed.

A slow hit that arrives on target long after the fight is over is as worthless as lightning-like shot that misses by a mile. What we must strive for is a balance between the speed of the shot and the accuracy of the hit. Let's discuss how to find that balance.

There are three parts to presenting the pistol and firing the shot. First is the movement of the pistol from the holster to the point position (on target). This must be done as quickly as humanly possible, regardless of the size of or distance to the target.

The second part is the time spent on the pause to verify the sight picture and its alignment on target. This is simultaneous with the prepping of the trigger. As the pistol arrives on target, the shooter must pause at the top of the stroke in order

Instead of trying to be fast, try to be smooth. Speed will come from smoothness, and smoothness will come from extensive and correct repetitions. Pay attention to small things, such as the line of travel from holster to target. Little things add up.

to prepare the trigger for discharge as well as to verify the sight picture. The time spent on this pause is greatly dependent on the difficulty of the shot. A large target at 3 meters requires relatively little sight picture verification, whereas a target at 50 meters will require considerably more verification time and a much more precise sight picture.

The final portion of the presentation is simply holding everything in place while the last ounces of pressure are applied to the trigger until the shot is fired.

In order to gain speed you must perform the correct procedure smoothly. This means excluding all unnecessary motion throughout the three parts of the presentation. It also means moving quickly from a position of rest.

The best way to develop the type of speed needed without sacrificing accuracy is to break the presentation down into its components and practice each one independently. In other words, in phase one you move the pistol up to the target as fast as possible without pressing the trigger. In phase two you prepare the trigger and verify the sight picture. In phase three you hold everything in place as you exert the final press on the trigger. Here are some dry practice exercises that will assist you in developing controlled speed.

EXERCISE 1

After following the dry practice safety procedures outlined in Chapter 6, set up the target at the appropriate distance. With as fast a movement as you can muster, present the pistol to the target. Make sure that you do not take any shortcuts that violate safety principles such as covering your support hand with the muzzle or touching the trigger too soon.

It is important that you do not press the trigger at this point. Continue the exercise until you can bring the pistol from the holster up to and aligned with the target in one second.

EXERCISE 2

Perform Exercise 1, but add preparation of the trigger and verification of the sight picture. As the pistol rises into the line of sight, the trigger finger takes up the slack on the trigger. When you arrive on target, do not let the trigger break. Control the trigger! Simultaneously, pick up the front sight through the rear sight notch. Close the nondominant eye and focus on the top edge of the front sight as it is perfectly aligned with the rear sight and superimposed on the target. Hold that position!

This drill takes the act of firing the shot right to the very edge of discharge. Hold the trigger prep and the sight picture for one to two seconds. Mentally think the words "pause" and "verify." Do not allow the trigger to break.

EXERCISE 3

Perform Exercise 2, taking the firing stroke to the very point of discharge. Mentally think the words "pause," "verify," and "press." As soon as you think "press," press carefully through that final stage of the trigger. Monitor the front sight for movement.

The first drill is lightning quick, almost as if you were intending to throw the pistol at the target. Exercise 2 teaches you to stop (pause) at the top of the stroke to verify sight picture and get the trigger ready to go. The trigger does not break in either one of these drills. It is important to emphasize that the final press is a distinct and different move from the actual presentation of the pistol. Exercise 3 puts it all together. When you think the word "press," you press through the final stage of the trigger pressure until the hammer or striker releases. Move up to that point as fast as you can and pause as long as you need in order to guarantee the shot. That is the secret to fast shooting. These drills can be conducted as live fire drills as well.

Only hits count! That is a statement that is as true as it is forceful. All of the tactical tricks and high-speed guns in the world will do you little good if you cannot hit on demand. Speed without accuracy is as valuable as a glass of water to a drowning man.

You are already familiar with the basics, the secrets of marksmanship. These are paramount to developing accuracy. Some self-appointed tactical gurus with little or no experience in personal combat will tell you that gunfights are close enough to not have to worry about accuracy. "Just hit him somewhere," they pontificate.

Excuse me? When you stop to consider the stresses that a man undergoes in a real fight, a fight to the death, it is clear that abandoning the principles of marksmanship is tantamount to suicide. Think back to your best day at the firing range. When you are shooting for blood (and your targets are doing likewise), you will only be *half that good!* Now if you always practice to "just hit him somewhere," the most important shot of your life will go—you guessed it—nowhere!

Take a page from the sniper discipline. Police snipers train to make eyeball shots at 100 meters. Their actual encounters are generally much closer and rarely require such precision. The idea is that if they are that accurate in training, the better they'll be able to place decisive shots on larger targets under stress. As long as realistic time intervals are adhered to, this is sage advice for pistoleros too.

Don't mistake the foregoing as advice to "accurize" your pistol. Your pistol is already inherently more accurate out of the box than you are. Instead, accurize your shooting technique. That is what will save you.

The following are some accuracy enhancing drills for you to practice. Note that these are live-fire drills that must be performed at the range. During these drills, your goal is to keep all of the shots touching each other. If they go into the same hole, you are on the right track. Remember, this is an exercise that develops a skill, much like push-ups and pull-ups develop arm strength. During tactical operations, we may settle for less in order to gain some speed. Developing the ability to fire a surgically accurate shot, however, will allow you to sacrifice relatively little when you "go fast."

DRILL 1

Set up a standard combat/humanoid target at 5 meters. Make a small aiming point on it, such as a cross or a dot, about an inch in size. Bring your pistol up to the point position and fire a group of five shots without taking your visual focus and attention off the front sight. Strive to place them all in the same hole or at least touching each other. Shoot slowly for accuracy only.

When 5 meters is no longer challenging, move to 7, and so on. Strive for as small a group as possible, and do not fire until every aspect of the sight picture and trigger press is perfect.

DRILL 2

Follow the same procedure as the previous drill, but begin in the ready position. Move from ready to point quickly, then carefully fire a single perfect shot. Do not rush.

DRILL 3

Follow the same procedure as the first drill, but begin with the pistol holstered. Remember, perfect shots only. Your group should be approximately the same size as the two previous exercises.

DRILL 4

Follow the same procedure as Drill 3, but fire two controlled shots. Press the trigger for the first shot. Hold the trigger to the rear on recoil and do not release it until you obtain a second sight picture. Now release it only as far as necessary to reset it for a second shot and again, focusing visually on the top edge of the front sight, press for the second perfect shot.

Once you can fire extremely accurate shots on demand, begin to include an increasingly shorter time interval. Your goal as a student of the pistol is to find your personal balance between speed and accuracy.

A Note About "Reading Your Targets"

It is sometimes difficult to gauge your performance at the firing range because of the noise and tumult associated with a live-fire drill. It is helpful if you look at your target as a final exam paper. It will tell you things about your grip, stance, trigger press, and so forth . . . if you know how to read it. Look at where your shots have hit. Assuming that your pistol is properly sighted in, any variance from a center hit is all you.

If you find that your shots are low on the target, it is a sign that you are not pressing the trigger carefully. Sometimes shooters will anticipate the shot and hurry the trigger press abruptly (AKA jerking the trigger). They may even reflexively force the muzzle down slightly in anticipation of the shot. This in turn causes the front sight to dip low and either to the left or right as the bullet leaves the barrel.

The training solution is to practice the "ball and dummy" drill. This drill is extremely useful, and I make it an ongoing part of my training. Fill a magazine two-thirds with dummy inert rounds and the remaining third with live cartridges, randomly interspersed. Now carry on with your training. Mentally convince yourself that the pistol is completely loaded with dummy rounds. The bulk of the trigger presses will bear this out. Eventually, however, you will experience a live round being fired and get a real surprise break. Prolonged use of this drill will desensitize you to the report and noise of the shot and will cure the flinch problem.

If you are a right-hander and your shots are consistently hitting the target to the right of the paper, you probably have too much finger on the trigger. The result is that when you press to the rear, you are also pulling to the right. You may think that everything is perfect, but the paper will not verify your feeling. If your shots are hitting too far to the left, invariably you are not placing enough finger on the trigger and causing the opposite of the previous situation. Note that a left-handed shooter will experience the same things. but to the opposite side of the target.

Shooting high is most often caused by not focusing intently enough on the front sight and instead looking up at the target at the final moment. It is also caused by not stopping on the target during a presentation and instead trying to "ambush" the target as you swing the pistol past it.

The solution is to maintain visual focus on the front sight as the shot is fired. In fact, look for the front sight lifting off the target on recoil. Additionally, be certain that you have in fact stopped moving before final pressure is exerted on the trigger.

CHAPTER 21

THE TRUTH ABOUT POINT SHOOTING

Trends come and go as the years pass. We've all seen the comical sketch where the wife, in the process of cleaning out her voluminous closet, asks the husband whether she should discard a particularly old dress. The husband's reply is to keep it, as it will eventually come back into style.

This phenomena of old issues revisited and coming back into vogue is prevalent not only in styles of clothing but in music and other aspects of our society. Oftentimes, it is the result of simple curiosity or even nostalgia. Other times, the motives are economic. Label anything properly and it will sell. "The answer to your problems" makes for a great deal of sales, especially if it offers an attractive shortcut.

In fashion or music, the worst that can occur from selecting something outdated is to be accused of having bad taste. In more serious pursuits such as police work or self-defense, the ramifications of selecting a new and improved method that is really old and substandard may be far more serious.

The topic in question, of course, is firearms training. There is a growing movement afoot to revisit the viability of point shooting, or unsighted shooting, as a replacement for the commonly accepted method of using the sights to align the weapon on an adversary.

Neither aimed fire or, as some call it, "instinctive" shooting are new. The question of which is better for combat, however, surfaces continuously. Each year we have a rash of new revelations on the subject. Recently, I had the privilege of attending a symposium for law enforcement firearms trainers hosted by a police standards group. A great deal of information was presented, much of it very interesting. The overall theme, however, seemed to be slanted toward the promotion of the instinctive/unsighted school of shooting and to the abandonment of proven principles which many of the presenters claimed as unrealistic.

For the sake of clarity, let's define a few terms. Point shooting is the use of the pistol in CQB environments against human adversaries without utilizing the sights in any manner to orient the pistol before or during the firing process. Sighted fire (as developed and taught by Jeff Cooper and his various students) refers to the use of the pistol in the CQB environment against human adversaries while using the sights to orient the pistol before and during firing.

The concepts of point shooting were taught in the police community for many years and as late as the 1970s. Due to the abysmal performance of police officers in gunfights, a better way was sought. Stop to consider that if point shooting actually worked as marvelously as its proponents claim, an alternative would never have been sought. Quite simply, too many officers were being killed by suspects after they missed them with unsighted fire at close range.

Some revolutionary individuals advocated point shooting up close but aimed fire as the distance increased. This created additional problems, not the least of which was that officers were still missing their shots at the close distances. The other problem was that introducing two distinctly different methods was a direct violation of Hick's Law, a scientific principle regarding human behavior under stress. In short, it states that if more than a single response is trained for a given stimulus, the subconscious mind must examine each one of those responses prior to reacting. Training point shooting for up close and aimed fire for distance resulted in drastically increased reaction times and complete failure under stress.

It was the failure of these ideas that led the warrior gunfighters of a generation ago to look for a better way. Their solution was the adoption of Jeff Cooper's system or one of its various derivatives. Many police agencies took this approach, abandoning the ineffective firearms training in place at the time (a big step) and adopting Cooper's techniques. If a large police department can do it, certainly smaller agencies and individuals can do so as well.

I am good friends with the firearms instructor of a large agency in Southern California. He tells me that in the last 30 years, that agency has had approximately 2,700 officer-involved shootings. I was told by one of that agency's senior officers that they had had, at one time, seven separate incidents where officers were killed by criminals whom they had missed at close range with pistol fire using the "old" methods.

Nobody wants to denigrate fallen officers, but if we are to learn from their mistakes we must analyze with a critical eye the circumstances of their last moments. The bottom line is that no one's tactics are always perfect. If the tactics are not perfect at the critical moment and the officer finds himself "going to guns," will his marksmanship skills save the day?

The answer for my friend's agency in the turbulent early years was a resounding and sobering no! But since abandoning the point shooting and sight-only-at-long-distance methodology in favor of the Cooper-based methods, their hit rate has risen dramatically. In the 1970s, the percent of hits per shots fired was abysmal. In 1991, after a number of years following the new program, the ratio rose to 56 percent. In 1996, it was 70 percent. I am told it is even higher now. This cause and effect has been repeated many times by agencies that have followed suit, to include military units as well as police departments.

Many point shooting advocates cite strong medical

The father of the modern technique and my personal friend, Jeff Cooper.

research data on the effects of stress on human combatants. They suggest that their methods are the only ones that will work under stress and the only ones really proven in actual combat. Some go further to suggest that those of us who've discussed the fine points of life and death with belligerent bad guys really didn't see the front sight after all but rather imagined the whole thing. Even claims of using unsighted point shooting techniques out to distances of 25 yards are made, with centered thoracic cavity hits no less!

The medical stress data given is invaluable, but depending on how it is interpreted it can be used to support either argument. As far as imagining the front sight rather than actually seeing it? Sorry guys: too many officers have used Cooper's method successfully to buy that one. In debriefings of gunfight winners, the question "Did you see the sights?" was invariably answered in the affirmative by those who hit and the negative by those who missed.

Many police officers who have not only seen the elephant but who collected the ivory as well have formulated some very serious ideas about winning a gunfight. These ideas do not include point shooting. Some of them are listed below:

1) Diligent training and an aggressive, pseudo-predatory attitude will dramatically mitigate the effects of stress. If a police officer can be trained to do his (or her) very complex job, that same officer can be trained to keep his cool and to operate his pistol effectively under stress, maximizing the accuracy of his shots by using the sights appropriately. To those who suggest that it cannot be done, the list of names of those who have done that very thing is long and distinguished. Granted, doing so is not easy; in fact it is damn difficult. But as one of the speakers at the recent P.O.S.T. Firearms Trainer Symposium said, "We are not animals, and we can get past that."

2) Another truth is that every shot you miss gives the other man yet another opportunity to kill you. Only hits count. To get hits by design, not by luck, you must use the sights. Some may be able to hit fairly well using point shooting in the controlled environment of a shooting range, but try the same thing in dynamic environments against shooting and moving opponents and missed shots will be the inevitable result. Anybody can get lucky (or unlucky). We seek to win by design, not by default.

3) Aggressive shooters will win every time over reactive defensive shooters. Those with cool, aggressive, warrior attitudes do much better than those with highly aroused, emotionally driven, victim attitudes. There is no possibility of victory in defense, but there is in the attack. The standard immediate action drill for an ambush is to assault the ambush. Gunfights are the same way. This is not say that we fix bayonets on our service pistols and charge in the face of danger but rather that our mental and emotional response to an attack must be to counter-

attack with greater violence. This attitude must be taught and cultivated. Being a victim is not a tactical option.

4) The sights must be used for all shooting except situations where you are so close that you can smell your adversary's bad breath and a standard firing position would allow him to grab and/or deflect your firearm. This doesn't mean that you spend second upon second watching a perfect sight picture. The degree of precision in sight alignment and the resulting sight picture is greatly dependent on the size of the target and the difficulty of the shot. This little tidbit is largely unknown to proponents of the notion that sighted shooting is "too slow." A large, close-range target requires very little precision, whereas the same target at 25 yards requires greater precision. An officer can easily be trained to accept what he sees of the sight or refine it based on the difficulty of the shot. This is far easier to teach, to learn, and to maintain than any so-called body index. Moreover, this will guarantee the placement of the shots and maybe even win the gunfight.

I urge those who are tempted to adopt point shooting to think long and hard before abandoning the Cooper technique and its derivatives. If the preceding argument was not sufficient to sway you, consider this. The next time you visit the range to train, look at your target. Instead of a two-dimensional silhouette, visualize a tall, muscular, tattooed, long-haired violent parolee who has sworn never to go back to prison and who wants to kill you for even suggesting the possibility. He's coming for you now, drool dripping from his fumanchu mustachioed face. You can see the hatred in his red eyes as he goes for the stolen and unregistered pistol in his belt. To survive, you must win, and to win, you must hit him solidly before he hits you. If you miss, you die. Now ask yourself this: do you feel lucky?

CHAPTER 22

FREQUENTLY ASKED QUESTIONS

I have been teaching for many years and in many countries—not as much as some of my older colleagues, but enough to have received a number of consistent questions from students. In this chapter I've tried to list the most common ones and answer them as I do in class.

1) *How often should I practice?*
   That depends on how good you want to get. Initially, to reach a high level of skill, frequent practice is necessary. This is especially true if you've recently attended a training course and learned new things. New skills must become ingrained in the subconscious with extensive repetition. Once such skills have become reflexive, intensive practice is not necessary. Daily practice is ideal, but every other day will still yield impressive results.

2) *How much time should I spend on a training session?*
   About 20 to 30 minutes is good. Some students will spend more time, and some less. Remember the goal: to ingrain perfect techniques into the subconscious mind. In order to do this, you need quality practice, not quantity practice. This also means intense and undivided concentra-

tion. As soon as you begin to feel tired or you find your mind drifting to other things, it is time to stop. Every repetition you do trains your neuromuscular connections as well as your mental focus. Doing it right a few times will yield better results than doing it poorly a thousand times.

3) *How fast should I train?*
Speed is a by-product of smoothness in execution. Smoothness, in turn, is a product of correct procedures ingrained into the neuromuscular and subconscious systems. Do not make the mistake of trying to intentionally go fast. Speed will come from practice.
 The speed you want is speed with control. Uncontrolled speed is a waste. When you train, begin with smooth and controlled, medium-speed repetitions. Eventually, these will smoothen even more as superfluous motions are eliminated.

4) *At what distance should I dry practice?*
The practice target should simulate the visual appearance of a man at 7 meters when placed 3 meters away. If you are attempting to develop long-range skills, then by all means extend the distance. If your dry practice training area is large enough to accommodate a life-size target at real world distances, all the better.

5) *What should I think about while practicing?*
What you focus on mentally is as important as what you execute physically. An important aspect of successful shooting is concentration. You must keep your eye and attention focused on the center of mass of the target while presenting the weapon. When the pistol is up in the line of sight and you are pressing the trigger, your attention and visual focus must be on the front sight. Think of what you are doing as you are doing it. Don't concern yourself with what you did a second ago or what you are going to do next. Rather, con-

centrate on the present action as you execute. Additionally, listen and focus on the commands given. These key words will become ingrained in your subconscious and eventually key you to the required physical responses.

6) *How often should I conduct live-fire training?*
Live fire is important to remind you what an actual shot feels and sounds like, but it should only form a minor part of your training. It is mere validation of your dry practice. To a degree, the more you shoot, the worse shot you become. One 30-minute session (about 50 to 75 rounds) every week or every other week is fine. But in the interim, you must conduct proper and consistent dry practice. Beware of schools and training programs that advocate voluminous amounts of shooting. Such activity will produce nothing but mountains of brass and poor skills.

7) *What should I practice when I conduct live fire?*
Practice the same drills you do when dry practicing. Use the same mental focus, follow the same procedures, and do them with the same attitude. Don't change a thing. You will soon find that your shooting is improving by the quality of your dry practice program.

8) *How do I overcome a flinch reaction?*
Flinching, or mashing the trigger, is a common ailment to shooters. Actually, it is either a reflexive forward push of the weapon after trigger press or a spastic jerking of the trigger. It comes from anticipating the shot rather than allowing it to surprise you every time. You must desensitize yourself to the report and blast of the shot.

The way to do this is to do more dry practice. Additionally, intersperse some dry practice in the live fire session, performing about three dry presses for each live shot. Strive for a perfect trigger press while concentrating on the front sight.

When this becomes comfortable, load a magazine a quarter full of live rounds and three-quarters of inert dummy rounds. Now you must tell yourself, and believe it wholeheartedly, that the pistol is loaded with dummy rounds and that it will not fire. When you bring the pistol up into a firing position and begin to press the trigger, focus intently on the sight picture and convince yourself that it will not fire. If there is in fact a dummy round in the chamber, the trigger press will be perfect without any subsequent movement of the front sight because of anticipation of the blast and recoil. If there is a live round in the chamber, you will experience a surprise break. When you experience a surprise break, you will always remember it. You must now strive to make each trigger press a surprise break. This will cure the post-ignition push and/or flinch.

9) *What about training courses that advocate 3,000 rounds a week?*

Again, to a certain degree the more you shoot, the worse shot you will become. Each shot you fire in training should be a perfect or nearly perfect and controlled shot. Otherwise you will be programming poor habits into your subconscious system. Perfect shots require perfect concentration. Firing such shots is, eventually, mentally fatiguing. There is a limit to anyone's ability to concentrate like that. Any shots fired after that limit has been reached are actually detrimental and wasted shots.

Sometimes in a training course, this limit must be pushed in order to cover all of the curriculum, but not without some concern over rest breaks and so on. Courses or instructors that advocate massive amounts of ammunition expenditure without the mandatory accompanying instruction are often concealing poor instruction or a lacking curriculum with the smoke and noise of ballistic self-delusion. Remember, any monkey can go to the firing range and mash the trigger 1,000 times in an afternoon, accomplishing nothing but making brass. It takes a thinking man to concentrate and to program perfect responses into his subconscious system. When life is the only prize, there can be no compromise!

10) *Will dry practice damage my guns?*
Absolutely not! Many of my personal firearms have seen hundreds of hours of dry practice training and are still going strong. If this is of concern to you, purchase one of the commercial orange plastic snap caps to cushion things.

A word of perspective: if your sidearm is so frail as to be damaged in mere dry practice, get rid of the damn thing and get a real pistol that will endure it.

SUGGESTED PRACTICE DRILLS

The following live-fire drill will give you some idea about the time intervals involved. It can be shot on any humanoid silhouette target and demands a realistic balance of speed and accuracy. Begin at the appropriate level for your skill (basic, intermediate, advanced, or instructor) and shoot this drill no more than three or four times a month.

1) Standard Exercises: single target, from holster, perform once

			Basic	Int.	Adv.	Inst.
a.	3 meters	two body, one head	1.5	1.3	1.2	1.0
b.	7 meters	two body, one head	1.7	1.6	1.5	1.3
c.	10 meters	two body	2.5	2.3	2.0	1.8
d.	15 meters	two body	3.0	2.7	2.5	2.3
e.	25 meters	two body	3.7	3.5	3.0	2.8
f.	50 meters	single shots	—	—	7.0	6.0
	Total shots for stage one:		12	12	13	13
	Possible score:		60	60	65	65

2) Multiple Targets: 5 meters away, targets 1 meter apart, center-to-center, one shot on each from holster, perform once

		Basic	Int.	Adv.	Inst.
a.	2 targets	2.0	1.7	1.5	1.2
b.	3 targets	—	2.0	1.8	1.5
c.	4 targets	—	2.5	2.0	1.8
d.	5 targets	—	—	2.3	2.0
e.	6 targets	—	—	2.6	2.3
	Total shots for stage two:	2	9	21	21
	Possible score:	10	45	105	105

3) Controlled Pairs: 7 meters on a single target, from holster, perform six times

	Basic	Int.	Adv.	Inst.
	—	1.5	1.2	1.0
Total shots for stage three:	—	12	12	12
Possible score:	—	60	60	60

4) Responses Right, Left, and Rear: 7 meter target, two shots each from the holster, perform once

		Basic	Int.	Adv.	Inst.
a.	Response Right	—	1.5	1.2	1.0
b.	Response Left	—	1.5	1.2	1.0
c.	Response Rear	—	—	1.5	1.2
	Total shots for stage four:	—	4	4	6
	Possible Score:	—	20	20	30

5) Small Targets at Close Range: head shot only, one shot only, from ready, perform each three times

		Basic	Int.	Adv.	Inst.
a.	3 meters	2.0	1.2	1.0	0.8
b.	5 meters	2.5	1.5	1.2	1.0
c.	7 meters	2.7	1.8	1.5	1.2
	Total shots for stage five:	9	9	9	9
	Possible score:	45	45	45	45
	Total shots for entire drill:	35	62	63	73
	Possible score:	175	310	315	365

DRY PRACTICE
TARGET

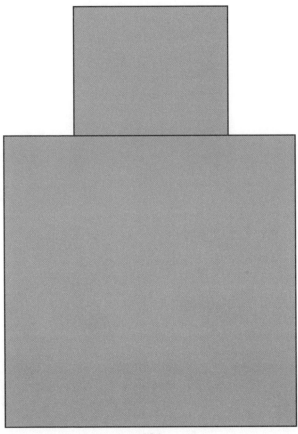

SUGGESTED READING LIST

Cooper, Jeff, *Principles of Personal Defense*, Paladin Press, 1989

– *To Ride Shoot Straight, and Speak the Truth*, Gunsite Press, 1988

Givens, Tom, *The Complete Guide to Concealed Carry*, Tom Givens, 1995

– *Fighting Smarter*, Tom Givens, 2000

Morrison, Greg, *The Modern Technique of the Pistol*, Gunsite Press, 1991

Suarez, Gabriel, *The Tactical Pistol*, Paladin Press, 1995

– *The Tactical Shotgun*, Paladin Press, 1996

– *The Tactical Advantage*, Paladin Press, 1998

– *The Tactical Rifle*, Paladin Press, 1999

Taylor, Chuck, *The Complete Book of Combat Handgunning*, Paladin Press, 1982

– *The Gun Digest Book of Combat Handgunnery*, DBI Books, 1997

ABOUT THE
AUTHOR

Gabriel Suarez is a veteran of Southern Californian law enforcement, where he has served for many years. His extensive field experience includes single officer patrol, gang enforcement, special operations, and tactical training. He was one of the founding members of his department's Special Weapons and Tactical Precision Rifle teams. In 1991 he was awarded the Police Medal of Valor for his actions during a critical incident. He is still active in the law enforcement profession and the training industry.